Matthew Fox

THE A.W.E. Project

ALSO BY MATTHEW FOX

A New Reformation!

*The Coming of the Cosmic Christ: The Healing of Mother Earth and
    the Coming of a Global Renaissance*

Confessions: The Making of a Post-Denominational Priest

Creation Spirituality: Liberating Gifts for the Peoples of the Earth

Creativity: Where the Divine and Human Meet

Hildegard of Bingen's Book of Divine Works with Letters and Songs (editor)

Illuminations of Hildegard of Bingen

In the Beginning There Was Joy

Manifesto for a Global Civilization (with Brian Swimmer)

Meditations with Meister Eckhart

*Natural Grace: Dialogues on Creation, Darkness, and the Soul
    in Spirituality and Science* (with Rupert Sheldrake)

One River, Many Wells: Wisdom Springing from Global Faiths

Original Blessing: A Primer in Creation Spirituality

Passion for Creation: The Earth-Honoring Spirituality of Meister Eckhart
    (formerly *Breakthrough*)

Prayer: A Radical Response to Life
    (formerly *On Becoming a Musical, Mystical Bear*)

The Physics of Angels: Exploring the Realm Where Science and Spirit Meet
    (with Rupert Sheldrake)

The Reinvention of Work: A New Vision of Livelihood for Our Time

Religion USA: Religion and Culture by Way of Time *Magazine*

Sheer Joy: Conversations with Thomas Aquinas on Creation Spirituality

*Sins of the Spirit, Blessings of the Flesh: Lessons for Transforming Evil
    in Soul and Society*

A Spirituality Named Compassion: Uniting Mystical Awareness with Social Justice

Western Spirituality: Historical Roots, Ecumenical Routes (editor)

Whee! We, wee All the Way Home: A Guide to a Sensual Prophetic Spirituality

Wrestling with the Prophets: Essays on Creation Spirituality

Matthew Fox

THE

A.W.E. Project

Includes DVD
by
Professor Pitt

Reinventing
Education

Reinventing
the Human

CopperHouse

Editor: Michael Schwarzentruber
Cover design: Margaret Kyle
Cover art: "Creativity," © copyright Javier Garcia Lemus. Used with permission.
Interior design: Verena Velten
Proofreader: Dianne Greenslade
Quotations from Ernest Becker, *Beyond Alienation: A Philosophy of Education for the Crisis of Democracy* (New York: George Braziller, 1967) used by permission of the publisher.

CopperHouse is an imprint of Wood Lake Publishing, Inc. Wood Lake Publishing acknowledges the financial support of the Government of Canada, through the Book Publishing Industry Development Program (BPIDP) for its publishing activities and acknowledges the financial support of the Province of British Columbia through the Book Publishing Tax Credit.

At Wood Lake Publishing, we practice what we publish, being guided by a concern for fairness, justice, and equal opportunity in all of our relationships with employees and customers. Wood Lake Publishing is an employee-owned company, committed to caring for the environment and all creation. Wood Lake Publishing recycles, reuses, and encourages readers to do the same. Resources are printed on 100% post-consumer recycled paper and more environmentally friendly ground wood papers (newsprint), whenever possible. A percentage of all profit is donated to charitable organizations.

Library and Archives Canada Cataloguing in Publication
Fox, Matthew, 1940-
    The A.W.E. project / Matthew Fox.
Includes bibliographical references.
ISBN 1-896836-84-4
    1. Education – Philosophy. I. Title.
LB14.7.F69 2006   370.1   C2006-903811-2

Published by CopperHouse
9590 Jim Bailey Road, Kelowna, BC, Canada, V4V 1R2
www.woodlakebooks.com
www.copperhousepress.com
250.766.2778

Printing 10 9 8 7 6 5 4 3 2 1
Printed in Canada by
Houghton Boston Printers, Saskatoon, SK

TABLE OF CONTENTS

PREFACE
A Crisis Called Education

People recognize that education is in trouble today. It is not just an American problem, as the Dalai Lama testifies when he says "Education is in crisis the world over." Is he correct?

The Dalai Lama is more of a global citizen than I am. The Dalai Lama hails from Tibet and has lived in India since his exile. He has also travelled the world, both the so-called first world and the so-called third world. He is an honest man and an insightful one. So when he tells us that education is in crisis the world over, I listen.

This I know and see daily. Education is truly in crisis where I live and work in the city of Oakland (where a new study from Harvard University found that 52 percent of high school students do not graduate), and in the state of California, and in the country of the United States. Bill Gates, chairman of Microsoft and a somewhat successful citizen, puts it bluntly when he says, "Our high schools are obsolete…they were designed 50 years ago to meet the needs of another age. Today, even when they work exactly as designed, our high schools cannot teach our kids what they need to know… Frankly, I am terrified for our workforce of tomorrow."[1]

I have lectured and studied enough in European countries to sense the crisis there as well. One professional counsellor I met recently, with a PhD in children's psychology, told me that time and again she sees in children today signs of Post Traumatic Syndrome caused by school itself! The symptoms of children wounded by education, she reports, are identical to those of soldiers traumatized by war itself. In other words, going to school often produces all the symptoms of having entered a battleground.

There is some comfort in learning from so wise a man as the Dalai Lama that the educational crisis we face is not just a local problem, or a North American problem, or even a European problem – it is a species problem.

But why is education in crisis the world over? It is a species problem because as a species we are between worlds. We are lost between the modern and the postmodern world and between the pre-modern or indigenous world and the modern and postmodern worlds. (Despite the concerted efforts of modern acts of genocide and slavery, wars and pogroms, the indigenous peoples of the world have not disappeared altogether but are very much with us in fact and in memory – in our blood and in the cells of our bodies.) As a species, we are in a deep crisis. We are an endangered species. We are endangering ourselves, our planet, our future. Yet we are also, as a renowned scientist recently said, "the one species that can prevent its own extinction."

But are we up to this task? Is our education up to this task?

I am writing this manifesto because I have been in the education field for my entire adult life and I have been busy about creating a pedagogy that is wisdom-oriented and not just knowledge-oriented. I believe wisdom is what young people and adults want. Unfortunately, neither young people nor adults are acquiring wisdom from most school systems. A recent study of undergraduates at UCLA found that more than 80 percent were unhappy with what they were receiving at the university.

A WORD ABOUT MYSELF

My interest in education goes back to the time I entered school at five years of age. From then until now, 60 years later, there has not been a year of my life when I was not in some

school or other as student or teacher or administrator or all of
the above. I have studied at the graduate level in three countries and have lectured in numerous countries and on several
continents, often to educators, as I did at Surry University in
London a year ago. In many respects, my education has been
alternative and somewhat out-of-the-box. That may be why
I feel inspired to speak frankly on the subject now.

What I present as solutions to an educational crisis in
these pages is not theory – it derives from a practice I have
been consciously involved in for 30 years. I first designed and
implemented an "Institute in Culture and Creation Spirituality" at Mundelein College, in Chicago. After seven years we
moved the program to Holy Names College, in Oakland, for
12 years; and then on to New College of California; and then
to Naropa University, Oakland. Over the years, the institute
has taken on new names, first becoming the University of
Creation Spirituality, and most recently, Wisdom University
in Oakland, California. The pedagogy we employ today has
been in effect with powerful results for three decades. My
programs have been a kind of teaching laboratory and this
book represents a summary of what we have learned. My desire now is to gift the young with what we have been learning
by experimenting with adults all these years.

I write this manifesto now because our species is at a
crossroads. Time is running out. We must reinvent the way
we are living on earth. Education and learning are a deep
and essential part of this change.

It is time to take this pedagogy from a uniquely adult learning situation (the schools we have operated until now have offered either a master's or a doctor of ministry degree) to learners of all ages. It is also time to utilize the media and technological advances to put forth an agenda that carries us beyond knowledge and power for power's sake, to wisdom and power for the sake of service and the community. Much of postmodern language – such as video, image-making, DJing and VJing, rap and spoken word, and break dancing – are forms of entertainment, but their implications for education are immense. Indeed it may be time to launch a new term, namely edutainment, and to start integrating these new and creative expressions into education itself.

While all of our graduates have been adults, many have gone back to teaching youth and designing programs for youth and writing books on youth education and even starting schools. In other words, what we have learned by teaching adults is profoundly applicable to young people today. Both adults and youth must be offered postmodern approaches to learning in these postmodern times. And postmodern wisdom includes the wisdom of pre-modern peoples.

One more personal note. I am now in my 66th year. I am entering my years as an elder. I do not want to be esoteric or academically fancy in putting forth what I have observed and learned as an educator during the past 35 years of my life. I want to put forth the core issues in a direct fashion. Thus, a manifesto.

Reinventing the human

Education is so pivotal for our species that one essential way to reinvent the species is to reinvent education. The opposite is also true: To reinvent education is to reinvent our species. The subtitle of this book is "Reinventing Education, Reinventing the Human." Allow me to give credit where credit is due; I owe the phrase "reinventing the human" to Father Thomas Berry, author of *Dream of the Earth, The Great Work,* and *The Universe Story.* I remember how struck I was by Berry's challenge, when he posed it a number of years ago at a lecture at our Institute in Culture and Creation Spirituality. Berry's vision is huge and it is also profound.

Nothing I have experienced since I first heard his call has diminished the truth of his prophetic announcement. Quite the opposite. The daily news about the melting of the ice caps; the thinning of the ozone layer which protects us from deadly solar radiation; the wiping out of the rainforests; the depletion of life in the oceans; the loss of topsoil; the disappearance of species, from elephants to chimpanzees to polar bears and many others, at alarming rates – none of this can be taken lightly. And it is all about our species and how our takeover of the planet has come at a very costly price for the earth, its creatures, and ourselves who seek to survive on the earth. Wars rage on and on, often in the name of religious ideologies. Corporate greed stalks the earth.

Clearly our reptilian brains coupled to our intellectual/creative brains have proven to be ravenous, and disastrous for the planet. Our greed needs taming. Our warlike nature needs taming. Our military expenditures need taming.

Yes, our education needs to catch up with our survival issues. And that is what this book is about: reinventing the human by reinventing education.

EDUCATION: AN ADULT ISSUE, NOT JUST A CHILDREN'S ISSUE

This educational crisis is not just a crisis about children. Imagining and executing the most perfect fourth grade classroom will not solve this crisis. This is an adult crisis as much as – and more than – it is a children's crisis. Children follow adults and if adults no longer know what it means to be adult, then surely children will not get the message either. If adults lack meaning in their lives, then children will be hard put to find it on their own. If adults quit learning, then children will find it a greater struggle to be empowered to learn.

When I use the word education I am not just talking about children. I am talking about everything adults learn, or think they have learned, and teach others, whether children, young adults, or one another.

After all, children return home from school to a house of adults – not only parents or stepparents, but grandparents, uncles, aunts, politicians, journalists, media moguls and personalities, clergy, and makers of film, television programs, and commercials. All adults are involved in education all the time. Children are watching. And learning. Or trying to.

Nothing is so natural as learning. Learning is to the mind what eating is to the body. It is a daily affair. It can be fun and delightful and delicious. It is also a necessity. Our minds close, our souls dry up, and our hearts shrivel when we are denied learning, just as our bodies shut down when they are denied the necessary nutrients food provides. Rabbi Abraham Heschel says, "Learning is not for life; learning is life." This means that when we cease to learn we cease to live. To be alive is to be learning. Sad to say, I have met many people – no few in positions of considerable power and responsibility – who long ago ceased to learn.

It also means that when we learn we fill up with life.

One proof that education is in crisis is that so few students or teachers or administrators find it fun anymore. Or delicious. Or playful. Or accessible.

I.
EDUCATION:
GIFT OR PUNISHMENT,
BLESSING OR CURSE?

One bias that renders education most pernicious is the presumption on the part of so many people that students do not want to learn, are not happy learning, are not happy period. Education, in this philosophy, has to be punishing. Education becomes a kind of vile medicine to take until you can escape school. Or a punishment for our sins (or for Adam and Eve's for that matter). Education is punitive, therefore.

If one begins with these presumptions, then one ends up with what we have: education as punishment, as enforcement, as cheerless and joyless. And education as exorbitantly expensive. Original sin is a self-fulfilling prophecy. If you begin in pessimism, you are very likely to end in pessimism.

This pessimism very much forged the modern consciousness. For example, René Descartes – one of modernism's most influential philosophers, whose influence on academia is still all pervasive in the West – operated out of fear and lost hope when, as a young man, his hero, the king of France, was assassinated.

If, however, you believe that learning is a treat, that truth and ecstasy go together, then education can be a blessing. Psychologist Ernest Becker addresses what he believes is the number one issue that separates educational philosophies. It is our philosophy of the human person. This is how he puts it:

> What, then, is the basic orientation for our curriculum; the single point from which everything derives…the unique vision that forms our whole course of study;… the one that awakens [a person's] most intense curiosity; the one that bathes [a person's] mind and electrifies it at the same time… What is this truth?
>
> It is the great Rousseau's truth; the one that caused him to fall swooning to the ground; the one over which he cried with hot tears of torment, joy, and discovery, soaking the whole front of his coat; the truth that he sobbingly flung out as a challenge to modern man; the truth that has been haunting us for two hundred years, and that is now ours to take up and use as a measure for all education – "Man is good."

Man is good; but society renders him evil. This was Rousseau's world-historical message. What is more suggestive as an orientation for education... This proposition is at the same time the single unifying principle for our whole curriculum. It is the natural principle of our whole general theory of alienation, the one that marks it as a genuine synthesis of knowledge.[1]

In my book *Original Blessing*, I teach that we are all blessings.[2] While this teaching infuriated the Vatican, I have demonstrated that it represents the oldest and surest teaching of Jewish spirituality, including the spirituality of the historical Jesus. Jews do not believe in original sin; neither do Muslims, Buddhists, indigenous peoples, Unitarian Universalists, or Eastern Orthodox Christians. Neither, I have found, do most parents.

It was Saint Augustine, writing at the time of the Christian takeover of the Roman Empire, who posited original sin. How strange that the Western church has preferred Augustine's teaching to that of Jesus and his Jewish, biblical ancestors for all these centuries. How strange that builders of empire, from Augustine's day to George Bush's day, have presumed original sin in the education of their subjects. But maybe it is not so strange after all. Maybe an original sin ideology is good for running an efficient empire. Maybe an original blessing education would empower too many people to question the state; to develop their critical and creative faculties; to move beyond guilt at being human, sexual, creative, and responsible; to let go of punitive parenting.

In his book *The Great Turning: From Empire to Earth Community*, scholar and financial expert David Korten calls the "true cultural war" that between a commitment to empire, which has preoccupied humans for 6500 years, and a commitment to earth community. He criticizes schools that prepare the young

> for obedient service to the institutions of Empire, but not for life and leadership in vibrant human communities nor for roles as social architects of a new human era. It is little wonder that so many youth rebel, drop out, and turn to sex, drugs, and violence in a desperate effort...to establish any kind of relationship that affirms their existence, even if in fleeting and ultimately self-destructive ways.[3]

Historian H. G. Wells put the issue this way 65 years ago:

> As mankind is, so it will remain, until it pulls its mind together. And if it does not pull its mind together then I do not see how it can help but decline... Our species may yet end its strange eventful history as just the last, the cleverest of the great apes. The

great ape was clever – but not clever enough. It could escape from most things but not from its own mental confusion.[4]

Is education part of our mental confusion – or part of our way out of it?

Korten believes that when empire replaced community as the goal of societies, we lost our way and distorted education as well as family life, economics, politics, and religion.

Traditionally, in both the Western biblical tradition and in Hinduism and the East, education has been understood as a "work of mercy or compassion," that is to say, as an avenue to relieving ignorance and lifting the veil of distorted relationships with reality. We might question whether education is lifting such veils of distortion today or actually contributing to them.

As we know, the word *crisis* in Chinese also means *opportunity*. The crisis in education and the crisis our species faces in regards to survival itself, are not only challenges but also opportunities that beckon us to rediscover who we are as a species, what it is we are doing here, what we want for our children and grandchildren, where we want to go from here, and how we intend to get there. In short, it is a moral issue. For morality is all about *where* we want to go and *what* means we choose to get there.

EDUCATION AS PATHOLOGY

Sometimes the cure for the disease of ignorance becomes worse than the disease. Many people have horror stories to tell about their experiences in school.

All education is adult education in its essence. Education is adults teaching children and adults teaching one another and adults teaching the upcoming generation. In that sense, education is truly a rite of passage in our culture and we recognize it as such at moments of ceremony, such as graduations, where professors and graduates alike don unusual ceremonial garb (like a priest saying Mass), everyone processes, music sounds, and prayers and uplifting talks (very much like sermons) carry the day.

For all of their ritual practices, universities can be dangerous places. I know one engineer in a major university who, after sponsoring a very successful, values-oriented conference on engineering and ecology, was physically attacked in the hallways of his university by an engineering colleague who could not take the mixing of morality, spirituality, and engineering that emerged at that conference. He was totally threatened by it.

It is as Ernest Becker said: "Today our universities breed competition, separateness, hate, war; we may call them whatever we will – 'hatcheries,' 'uni-nurseries' – but not universities. That institution has not yet dawned in any land on this planet."[5] A true university would teach peace and community by example, for it would awaken all within its purview to the joy and meaning of being part of the universe, indeed a thinking and praising part of the universe.

Biologist David Orr of Oberlin College writes about the piecemeal consciousness of the university today.

> We have fragmented the world into bits and pieces called disciplines and subdisciplines, hermetically sealed from other such disciplines. As a result, after 12 or 16 or 20 years of education, most students graduate without any broad, integrated sense of the unity of things. The consequences for their personhood and for the planet are large.[6]

Stanford educator Mark Gonnerman calls for a "uni-versity" instead of a "multi-versity." As far back as 1956, Kenneth Boulding observed that

> the universe of discourse is crumbling into a multiverse, and in one's more depressed moments one looks forward to a time when the progress of science will grind to a standstill in a morass of mutual incomprehensibility. Out of our intellectual pride, we may be building a new Tower of Babel.[7]

Becker puts the case bluntly when he says,

> The great stumbling block is the modern university
> itself. It is not a seat of learning. No matter how wide
> the doors are thrown open, how many new accom-
> modations are built, how much scholarship money
> is voted by Congress and the states, the terrible fact
> remains: The American University exists to shape
> candidates for the jobs of the American commercial-
> industrial system. It is a professional and vocational
> institution, not truly an "educative" one. It is a place
> where one spends four or more years mechanically
> earning the right to fill the better available jobs. It
> is education for society as it now stands rather than
> for the ideals of a society as it might better it. It is
> higher learning conducted as a business...conducted
> according to the best rules of automatically function-
> ing bureaucracy, as Max Weber predicted.[8]

MODERN EDUCATION: MEANINGFUL OR MEANINGLESS?

Meaninglessness raises its head everywhere in our times.
Workers in Scandinavia and other places count meaninglessness as their number one problem. What I have learned from
the strong response to my book *The Reinvention of Work* is
the omnipresence of meaninglessness in our times. People are

looking for meaning in their work, meaning in their lives, and they are not getting it. At a conference of cultural leaders I chaired in Finland, and at a gathering of labour and management I addressed in Geneva, the same subject arose. Studies indicate that even when one's salary and retirement are assured, as they are in some European countries – perhaps especially when that is the case – depression and meaninglessness haunt the worker. Studies among workers in Germany found that the greatest cause of absence from work was depression.

Since universities are training grounds for workers, we can pose the question: Do schools educate for meaning or for meaninglessness?

I have learned the following lesson since launching our own university as a response to my study on work (for we cannot reinvent work without reinventing education, which is so often the incubator for work): When creativity and cosmology are part of education, meaningfulness returns. Indeed, many "recovering workers" – academicians, engineers, social workers, therapists, artists, clergy, business people, and others – entered our program with weary souls, but emerged "reborn" and awakened and reinvigorated and recommitted to their vocations. I believe that our pedagogy, which has been in the making for 30 years, has proven itself time and again to work, to instill meaning and inspire students to begin life and work anew with vigour and a deeper purpose.

Becker says that "with man, meaning has become conscious; his conception of life determines how he sees all its parts... Man is the meaning-creating animal."[9] If we are the "meaning-creating animal," then do our educational efforts fulfill their task? Is meaning being inculcated? Is meaning being educed in our educational program, from grade school through professional schools? What meanings are we eliciting, are we passing on?

Meaningful is an interesting word. In English, it is like the word *grateful*. The implication is that there is no half measure to either meaning or to gratitude. You either have it or you don't. Your life is either meaningful or meaningless. You are either grateful or thankless. Do we live in a culture that robs us of meaning? Does it have to be this way? Are we educating our children in less and less meaningful ways? Do we have to?

Does meaninglessness begin in education itself? Becker analyzes the situation this way.

> The problem of meaninglessness in modern life...is not a problem of absolute meaninglessness, but of relative meaninglessness – of constriction, narrowness, limited scope and horizon; of a world-view that calls upon energies that are too shallow, too facile, too inverted to a humdrum daily quest. Modern man's meaninglessness is a problem of what to do with life, what to do with it beyond simply living it out in a completely fetishized way. It is a problem, to use Augustine's example, of not looking up, of

not looking deeply... Niko Kazantzakis confessed, he too was launched in this same search for peace of mind through highest possible meaning, and he did not find it until he found that his work and life were grounded in the deepest purposes of creation... What can happiness mean for man, except to realize that life is a gift, and not a burden?

This is why modern man whines so pitifully with the burden of life – he has nothing ultimate to dedicate it to; nothing infinite to assume responsibility for; nothing self-transcending to be truly courageous about. He has only himself, his dazzling and diverting little consumer objects; his few closely huddled loved ones; his lifespan; his life-insurance; his place in a merely biological and financial chain of things.[10]

I agree that the modern mentality is a "whining" mentality. I also find many academicians who are whiners and complainers. They are often prima donnas who do not expect to serve life, but expect life to serve them. Patriarchy generates whiners. I find academicians who love to think of themselves as "postmodern deconstructionists" but who take absolutely no effort to *reconstruct*. Such persons whine and complain, and raise the sounds of cynicism to a whole new art. Like children, they can take things apart but they cannot put anything together. They expect fat salaries and guaranteed wages (i.e., tenure) just because they show up for work.

I also observe among young people that the postmodern mentality can move, and desires to move, far beyond whining. It wants fun and at its best it wants justice and great dreams that make justice happen. It wants a bigger canvas on which to live life more fully.

The modern age instructed us for knowledge and knowledge skills and that is no mean accomplishment. We can erect bridges that remain steady, and build airplanes that transport us around the globe at unheard of speeds; we can launch rockets that take us to the moon, and take our instruments to Mars and the moons of Titan and to far corners of the Milky Way. And those are wonderful accomplishments!

But the modern age did not give us meaning. Meaning comes from traditions of *wisdom*, not from traditions of knowledge. The pre-modern world was far better at meaning than was the modern world. And its education was geared toward meaning.

So our task today is to incorporate pre-modern wisdom and meaningfulness into our vast store of modern knowledge. Is education up to the task? Not education as we are currently practising it, obviously. We are talking here about form, about putting new wine in old wineskins (or old, rich wine in new wineskins). The forms of modern education actually exclude meaning. But ancient forms show us the way. Forms of ritual, of art, of meditation, of celebration, of remembering, of chanting, of what psychologist Otto Rank calls the "irrational."

At this time in history, the indigenous people of South America are asking and praying to "change the dreams of the North." That is, the industrial dreams, the consumer-driven dreams that are driving our economy and that are despoiling the earth and thereby our future as a species. What are the dreams of our educational systems? Are we dreaming old dreams, tired dreams, dreams that you must lose if I am to win? Can we change the way education dreams? Can we dream the kind of dream that Sharif Abdullah dreams when he writes of "creating a world that works for everyone"?[11]

MOVING BEYOND MISEDUCATION TO
MINDFUL EDUCATION

The problem and crisis that education lays before us is this: "miseducation" is as possible as good education. Miseducation is education that fails to *educe*, to lead out of (Latin: *e ducere*) individuals their best and noblest capacities – our capacities for joy and wonder; awe and sharing; biophilia, justice, and compassion.

Is our education mindful or mindless? Does it contribute to filling the person with wonder, confidence, and empowerment? Or to alienating the learner and disempowering him or her? A mindful education would, for example, increase our capabilities for silence, for stillness and contemplation. It would enhance our capacity for grappling with chaos and for living with stress; our capacity for letting go, for letting be, and for forgiveness. It would grow our capacity for creativity, as well as our relationship to our lower chakras, from which spring our love of the earth, and our capacity for compassion, and for passion and moral outrage and for steering them to positive use. This is what mindfulness accomplishes. Anything less than this is mindless education.

Mindful education addresses what Thomas Aquinas calls "the human's noblest act," that is, joy. Yes, joy and education ought to go together. We ought to be learning our noblest capacities, and nurturing them and developing them. This, too, is part of a mindful education.

Where miseducation reigns there is a kind of sickness. Education as pathology, one might call it. The sickness extends to family and community, and to the culture itself (which Clarissa Pinkola Estes defines as "the family of families"). When education becomes pathological, costs skyrocket, for no one is happy at work and they must be compensated not with the rewards of the work but with paycheques. There is unhappiness and burnout. There are suicides and there is boredom. There is lack of joy. There are power trips, including "adultism," wherein adults – cut off from the child inside – resent the young and lord over them because they are young. There is a lack of elders and there is knowledge at the expense of wisdom. Only one-half of one chakra gets educated; the other six and one-half get ignored, including the heart, moral outrage, creativity, compassion, relation to the cosmos and to the earth. We will deal with character and chakra development more in chapter 5 below.

Education's problems are not to be found so much in unions or teachers or tax programs, as such, but in our universities, where adults are too often mistrained about life, work, and learning. From the university there is launched a kind of trickle-down miseducation.

Therefore, the cure lies in the university itself. The university must cure itself.

While the problem we face is global and species-driven, the reality is very local. One political genius in the American congress said that "all politics is local."

I believe that all education is local, if for no other reason than it concerns our children, our taxes, our community, our gifts, our time, our learning. In addition, we all have opinions about education.

Every adult, every citizen, also has horror stories – or happy stories – about school. Educational abuse is a reality. It ought to be examined and talked about. A kind of sado-masochism can easily prevail in places of upper education and when it does such abuse is often passed on to the next generation, a phenomenon that follows the pattern of sexual abuse of children. When education becomes punitive, intervention is called for.

Fortunately, there are alternatives, such as awe-based instead of punitive-based education. We will discuss this in greater detail below.

Janet Holmgren, who is president of Mills College, a liberal arts college for women in Oakland, California, commented recently that "higher education is remarkable for being the most conservative institution in our society." That is a telling statement. Maybe it is time for a change. Education is a place to conserve, learn, and respect the past; but it is also a place that needs criticism, particularly self-criticism, as well as dreams and goals, to shape the future, and to unleash the creativity and moral imagination to make that new future come about.

Education is so important to our culture that to neglect to criticize it is tantamount to not caring about it. Education must find a rhythm between being "in the world" and being "apart from the world." It is not meant only to conserve, but also to *inspire*. And to serve, not just conserve.

Money and education

Money is an issue in education, but it is not the core issue. Our financial attitude toward education is more like a canary in a mine, a signal of how much we really value our children when we refuse to support education. One's budget usually reflects one's priorities.

Robert Freeman was a businessman in the computer industry for 20 years. He had risen to vice president of marketing in a major company when he quit and chose to teach economics and history in Los Altos High School instead. As a teacher, he learned that education is harder than business "because cultivating human intelligence is one of the most difficult things in the world. It is far more complex and takes far longer than producing cheaper widgets or staging new ad campaigns." While efficiency guides decision making in business, "it is a disaster for producing intelligence and character in children. Remember, intelligence and character come from carefully managed complexity, ambiguity and uncertainty, all delivered in a safe, patient, nurturing environment. This is the opposite of efficiency." Good teachers, he points out, "are expensive, as well they should be. They possess a magical combination of empathy, intelligence, ingenuity, patience and persistence – the very traits we're trying to develop in our children." When we refuse to spend money on schools, we turn away the hope of the children themselves.

Freeman puts the question:

How many parents are willing to turn their children over to companies whose principle goal is to make a profit off them? How many want them taught by the cheapest teachers, crammed into the largest classrooms, reciting only the most rote repetition? Yet, if it is to make a profit, that is the only plausible vision that mass privatized education has to offer us: McStudents.[12]

A MANIFESTO DEDICATED TO AROUSING
THE NEED TO TEACH THE IGNORANT

I have been making the point for some time now that our culture is so off-centre that we have in great part separated justice from law, commerce from stewardship, religion from spirituality, and education from learning. Other than that we are in great shape! Can we bring learning and education together again? That is the theme of this manifesto.

This book is a kind of manifesto because it is direct and blunt and passionate. I am passionate because we are discussing a very important topic, the future of our species as portrayed by the forms of education we promote and tolerate. It is blunt because time is running out on our species – there is no time to waste, no time to beat around the bush. Lester Brown of the World Watch Institute believes that we have only nine years left to change our ways as a species, or the ecological damage we are doing will sink us.

Also, to be honest, time is running out on me. After 35 years of teaching adults, I want to lay bare what I have learned about alternative education and how we can apply those lessons learned with adults to the younger generation. As I find myself halfway through my 66th year, I am aware that time is running out on me. Now is the time to pass on what I have learned about education to a younger generation. This is what elders do.

What is a manifesto? The word comes from the French word to *manifest* or *make manifest*. Synonyms for manifest are "obvious," "evident," "easily understood or recognized." According to the *Webster's Dictionary*, a manifesto is a "public declaration of intentions, motives or views." I want here to make public and clear my intentions, motives, and views about education. Is what is *manifest* also *clear*, and *making manifest making clear* what is hidden? A kind of revelation, therefore, or a lifting of the veil?

Today we are all ignorant. This is great news! No one has all the answers. No one individual and no one tribe, no one religion and no one culture, no one nation and no one economic system has all the answers – and no one practice of education. As a species, we are on the verge of either something profoundly deep and new (which incorporates deep truths from the past) or of extinction itself. We can choose. As citizens, as actors on this cosmic stage called Mother Earth, we can choose.

Ignorance is universal. We all arrive quite ignorant. Each human being comes into the world quite ignorant. It is part and parcel of mothering and fathering to relieve that ignorance. It is the culture's task to relieve that ignorance as well. It "takes a village" after all.

Everyone, in some respect, has an opinion about education (just as we all have opinions on economics, politics, and religion). Education is a universal phenomenon after all. We have all either attended school or dropped out of school; liked school or hated it, or found some middle ground. Most of us have children in school or dropping out of school; going on for more education or not; liking it or not. Our taxes go to education, our politicians sound off on it; our charity money may go to support it. Many people work in educational settings and a good number of people vote for members on school boards to represent them, or attend PTA and school meetings on behalf of their children. Many of us work directly or indirectly in education – business people and other professions are deeply affected by the quality of graduates who come to work in their world. So education affects us all.

All the spiritual traditions of the world honour education, considering it a spiritual practice for learner and teacher alike. The prophet Isaiah in the Hebrew Scriptures lists it among the works of compassion. The Christian church, following suit, names "teaching the ignorant" as one of the spiritual works of mercy. Education is a spiritual act, an essential work of compassion. Hinduism teaches the relief of ignorance as the path to enlightenment. The Buddha, too, saw human travail as being caused by ignorance and enlightenment as the way beyond ignorance. All indigenous peoples had their special ways – always including ceremony or ritual – to teach the young their place in community, their place in the cosmos.

Rabbi Heschel says that we must educate "not just the mind but the soul." The modern era practically threw out the word soul, banished it from educational discourse altogether. The results are everywhere to be seen. Education has become in many instances quite soulless. This lack of inner awareness breeds anthropocentrism, misogeny, materialism, greed, competition, "consumeritis," rationalism, and power games. It sets us up as passive citizens to serve the empire, as Korten puts it. The modern era has practically assassinated the meaning of education in the West.

Education can be fixed. A search for wisdom – not mere knowledge – is long overdue.

We have illuminated some issues in the crisis that is education today. A global crisis it is. Now, and for the rest of this book, we will explore medicine for our ailing educational efforts. We will do so in four stages designated as A.W.E., or Ancestral Wisdom Education. These stages include the following:

1. **Awe-Based Education**
2. **A: Ancestral-Based Education**
3. **W: Wisdom-Based Education**
4. **E: Education – 10 Cs to Balance the 3 Rs**

2.
THE A.W.E. PROJECT:
AWE-BASED EDUCATION

I propose that the appropriate medicine for our postmodern educational ailments is a healthy dose of A.W.E. Awe in this context is both the experience of awe, which we will discuss in this section, and the more specific breakdown of the term A.W.E. into its constitutive parts of Ancestral Wisdom Education. The latter will be treated in chapters 3, 4, and 5 below.

WHY AWE, WHY NOW?

The modern era was not big on awe. It was more dedicated to taming awe than fanning it; more intent on mining what was awesome than praising it. More intent on making money than on making awe. Those who make awe for us, artists for example, are rarely honoured in a commerce-driven society – until, of course, they become makers of big money. Then their work is discovered because it serves financial interests, not because it serves the interests of awe itself.

Ernest Becker comments on this quality of the modern worldview:

> This is the tragedy that Western commercialism and communistic collectivism share in full and equal partnership. Each has lost man in its own way because each has lost the full meaning of the individual life. Man, then, needs a living and daily concern with ultimates, with the mystery of being, and with his role in the perpetuation of being. And rational, technical knowledge, as we said, cannot give this… Man needs nothing less than a full world picture; *and ancient man – unlike modern man – had not yet lost his awe of nature and being.*[1] (italics mine)

Unlike the modern world, the pre-modern world was very at home with awe, as Becker observed. "Ancient man had not yet lost his awe of nature and being." Indeed, pre-modern humans were thunderstruck by daily awesome encounters with the heavens and stars, the planets and the seasons, the animals and the plants, the wonders of everyday existence.

This awe found its way into ceremonies and rituals, where, for example, dances that celebrated the awesomeness of combing one's hair in the morning, or of finding food or preparing it or eating it, of dressing and cooking and cleaning, were celebrated.

In our postmodern times, we need to draw on some of this pre-modern energy, for we all have both a modern and a pre-modern soul in us and our pre-modern souls are starved for awe and for wonder. This is what makes us young and allows us to identify with the young – our capacity for awe and wonder. Rabbi Heschel put it this way: "The beginning of our happiness lies in the understanding that life without wonder is not worth living. What we lack is not a will to believe but a will to wonder."[2]

A "will to wonder" – now there lies a different under-standing of will. Not will as power, or will as gritting one's teeth, or will as shouting and barking orders over others, or will as "I know I can, I know I can," but will as wonder. Will as wonder is a child's will, a will of eagerness to learn, a will of desire to be seduced, amazed, broken open; a will of expanding, growing, exploding. Jesus said something similar when he said, "Unless you turn and become as children you will not receive the reign of God." Receptivity. Receptivity is more alive in children than in adults. Adults need to relearn wonder and the awe that goes with it.

And education does, too.

But education will only relearn wonder and awe when adults do so. The opposite of awe – the cynicism of "I have seen it all before" and "nothing can amaze me" and "I dare you to make me childlike and enthusiastic again" and "I hate your enthusiasm" – this cynicism very much rules the day today. Much of what we call "news" is based on it and invested in it. An emphasis on exams and grades is not an emphasis on awe.

SCIENCE AS A SOURCE FOR AWE AND WONDER

British biologist Rupert Sheldrake observes that science teaching today is 50 years behind the times. In other words, students are learning 50-year-old science in 50-year-old ways. That eliminates awe.

Sheldrake cites Sir Karl Popper, a philosopher of science, who has said that through modern physics materialism has transcended itself. But has this reality entered into the classroom? Sheldrake comments:

> The image of science that most people have is at least fifty years out of date and often a hundred years out of date. There is no good reason, other than habit, why we should go on teaching an outmoded scientific ideology to children in schools.[3]

But cutting awe out of the "ideology of science" will prevent a new (and more ancient) grasp of science to occur.

Yesterday's science was mechanistic and passed on the news that the universe was inanimate and without purpose, soulless and without meaning. Yet "academic biology and medicine are still under the sway of the mechanistic world-view, living fossils of an older mode of thought," laments Sheldrake.[4]

The reality is that science is itself busy being struck by awe these days. Consider the childlike enthusiasm expressed by NASA scientists when the modules it had landed started roaming on Mars. To me, part of the wonder of the occasion, in addition to the amazing photography from this red planet, was seeing the joy of the technical team that made the landing possible. The same occurred recently with the landing of a space probe on the largest of Saturn's moons, Titan. There was a palpable joy and childlikeness – an awe therefore – among the scientists explaining the photos we were seeing.

How do we relearn awe and redo education? We make awe a priority in our lives and in our worldview. We care about praising again. Small things are very awesome indeed. The cells of our bodies, for example.

One scientist who is busy reinventing herself and her profession by regaining awe as a priority is Sondra Barrett. Barrett has brought awe into her life by asking different questions about her specialty, biology, and by connecting biology to photography so that she and others can actually meditate on the awesome wonder of the cell itself.

Barrett talks about the cytoskeleton, the vibrating dynamic matrix of the cell, as the true mastermind of cell intelligence, which helps manage and coordinate cellular operations. How significant is the work of the cytoskeleton?

> Just consider what intelligence it takes to develop an entire cell. And what about the construction and coordination of communities of cells? If we were going to construct a vast community we'd hire a city planner and architect to draw up the plans. We'd also need a master coordinator to decide what to build first. In cellular communities, our genes are the plans, the cytoskeleton the coordinator and mastermind.

Cells, it turns out, are so committed to serving the whole body that some actually "choose" to self-destruct, thus benefiting "the community to make available more room and food for the rest." Cells stretch out to grow; they ball up to die; and they collect themselves "just right" for the purpose of maturation. The cell must balance tension and forces in order to survive. This process is called tensegrity, an architectural term for both tension and integrity. "Tensegrity refers to any physical structure or system that stabilizes and supports itself by balancing opposing forces of tension and contraction."

Living with tension! Balancing forces of contraction and

expansion, tension and rest – isn't that what we have to do all our lives? What lessons our cells have to teach us.

Among the "amazing powers" that Dr. Barrett sees within our cells are an invisible, integrating intelligence embedded in their vibrating architecture; a "seeing eye" electromagnetic infrared energy; an ability to shapeshift opposing forces and mind states; and directed movement. Barrett sees love and compassion occurring in the cells themselves, insofar as they reach out and open, expand and let go. She comments: "The Sufi mystic Rumi talks about the Beloved as Divine. Perhaps our cells hold us as Beloved. Can we behold them as beloved? What greater wisdom is there than that…"[5]

DEVELOPING A DAILY DOSE OF AWE

We carry awe with us daily and we need the help of scientists and teachers to awaken that awe. I attempted to provide a "litany of blessing" of the awe of our flesh in my book on flesh and spirit called *Sins of the Spirit, Blessings of the Flesh*.[6] I offer here a brief summary of the facts I gathered. They belong to all of us. They are awe reaching out to shake us up and wake us up today. They ought to provide the substratum for all learning and all education – learning is itself one of the truly awesome activities of the universe. And we are in the middle of it! (How dare we render learning boring and call it "education." Shame on us!)

Here are some facts staring us in the face, if we only listen.

☞ Matter is frozen light and for every molecule of light that is matter there are a billion particles of light that are not matter. This means matter is rare and special – we are incarnated light.

☞ Sixty percent of the matter of our bodies is made up of hydrogen atoms, which were present in the first years of the fireball, 13 billion years ago.

☞ The remaining 40 percent of our bodies is made up of atoms forged in the stars about 5.5 billion years ago.

☞ The human body holds 100 trillion cells each with 100 trillion atoms in them. Together they produce enough light to illuminate a baseball field for three hours with one million watts of floodlight brilliance.

☞ While the nine planets began with the same elements, all geological activity came to halt on four of them within one billion years, and on the other four hardly anything evolved at all. Only Earth was the proper size so that a balance between gravity and electromagnetic energy happened and with it complex molecules for life.

☞ Thanks to the moon, the entire North American continent rises six inches during the new and full moons.

☞ Some of the dust we breathe daily is as old as our solar system – 4.6 billion years old.

☞ One million earths can fit inside the sun.

☞ The sun emits more energy in one second than humankind has consumed in the whole of its history.

☞ Our Milky Way galaxy represents one trillionth of the universe.

☞ Topsoil is 50 percent air. The soil actually inhales oxygen and exhales carbon dioxide down to a depth of several feet.

☞ In summer, an average-sized tree gives off a ton of water every day.

☞ There are prairie grasses in the Midwest whose roots are 10,000 miles long.

☞ A single rye plant's roots grow over three miles per day in search of food.

☞ The human heart weighs only half a pound, but it does the daily work-equivalent of lifting a ton from the ground to the top of a five-story building

☞ Stomach acid is so powerful it can dissolve razor blades in less than a week. The stomach produces a new lining every three days to protect itself from its own acid.

☞ Fat is 88 percent carbon and hydrogen, which makes it chemically very close to gasoline and other hydrocarbon fuels.

☞ Our bones are one of the strongest building materials known to man. They can withstand stresses of 24,000 pounds per square inch, or about four times that of steel or reinforced concrete. Yet they live and grow back when they are broken.

☞ The sky is actually the air we breathe and walk in every day.

☞ One square inch of human skin contains 19 million cells, 625 sweat glands, 90 oil glands, 65 hairs, 19 blood vessels, 19,000 sensory cells and more than 20 million microscopic animals.

☞ African bushmen can see four moons of Jupiter with the naked eye and can hear the sound of an airplane approaching them from as far as 70 miles away.

☞ Humans hear frequencies as high as 20,000 hertz (vibrations per second) but dolphins hear frequencies as high as 280,000 hertz.

☞ Our mammalian brain is the fastest developing organ in evolutionary history.

☞ Each second over 100,000 chemical reactions occur in the brain. The brain produces more than 50 psychoactive drugs, which affect memory, intelligence, sedation, and aggression.

Surely these scientific facts are worthy of arousing awe, wonder, and praise. They are perfect material for young people to celebrate through song, poetry, rap, theatre, music, video, and more. These facts could provide the content for the new language of rap and video and music-making, which our technological revolution has made available to youth. Youth are at home with these new forms, but they deserve elders who will teach them healthy *content*. Otherwise, lacking healthy content with which to fill their spirits or souls, they experience only discontentment, and the content of their songs and poetry derives from anger alone and not from deeper places of awe and gratitude.

We live, move, and have our being in these realities, just as we carry all the mystery and wonder of our cells around with us. I cannot imagine the young of every age and every class – but especially the materially dispossessed and disadvantaged – not responding joyfully to these facts and figures. These awesome realities can awaken interest in learning all over again. And the beauty of the response that is sure to follow might set hearts aflame and launch a new renaissance from the ground up.

Why is education not arousing youth to such creativity and gratefulness? Are we all busy learning and relearning the role of awe in our lives? If not, why not? Perhaps it is because adults, including teachers and superintendents and educational structures, are no longer struck by awe. They are old and senile and goat-like. Maybe they need to go back to school – not to modern schools whence they were originally educated, but to wisdom schools where awe is on the agenda.

It is essential that all teachers and indeed all adults learn such awe-filled truths about their lives. Without awe, we are low in energy and we have little of importance to pass on to the young.

With awe, one is filled with praise. And that makes all the difference.

What if education became praise-based? Awe-based? What would change? Wouldn't everything change, including our level of joy in our learning process and in our learning spaces?

AWE AND IMMENSITY

The poet Goethe observed in the 19th century that "in awe one feels profoundly the immense." Awe carries with it deep and profound feelings. We do not readily forget our experiences of awe. Awe introduces us to the Immense. Awe is the door, the portal, the threshold to immensity.

How important is that? Years ago, J. B. Phillips wrote a book entitled *Your God Is Too Small*. I would propose that an epitaph on our species, should we go extinct, be the following: Your World is Too Small; Your Soul is Too Small. We do have to grow our minds, our hearts, our worlds – and this is what awe helps us do. It stretches us, takes us to the edge, to the horizon, to the Beyond where our imaginations can truly breathe, grow wings, and soar. Maybe we should respell education as "edge-ucation" – taking us to the edge. If it does not do that for us, it is failing us. As a species, we are *capax universi*, "capable of the universe," in the words of Thomas Aquinas. We are an edgy species – we want to grow, to expand, to travel to the edge – and awe is our ticket to that great vision.

One writer has pointed out that immensity dwells within all of us. But we need solitude to allow it to emerge in all its power and beauty. Furthermore, immensity awakens both *intimacy* and *intensity* or energy. French philosopher Gaston Bachelard writes, "We discover that immensity in the intimate domain is intensity, an intensity of being, the intensity of a being evolving in a vast perspective of intimate immensity."[7] Who among us does not want to so evolve? To grow insofar as we are capable into a vastness that is both immense and intimate?

Awe assists with that journey. It is food for the journey. Fuel for the journey. No food, no fuel.

What follows from such encounters with immensity? "Slowly, immensity becomes a primal value, a primal, intimate value. When the dreamer really experiences the word immense, he sees himself liberated from his cares and thoughts, even from his dreams. He is no longer shut up in his weight, the prisoner of his own being."[8] Awe liberates.

Awe and love go together. It is difficult if not impossible

to feel awe and not feel love. Derek Walcott, a Caribbean poet who won the 1992 Nobel Prize for poetry, said in his acceptance speech, "For every poet it is always morning in the world. History a forgotten, insomniac night. History and elemental awe are always our early beginning, because the fate of poetry is to fall in love with the world, in spite of History."

Thus we learn that "elemental awe" starts things over for us, brings us back to our origins, connects us to the beginnings, makes us young again. And out of this youthfulness love happens; we fall in love again – not with history, for history is so cruel, but with "the world," with being itself, with Life and all its promises. Awe overcomes history. Awe overrides pain, suffering, injustice, and mistreatment. And poetry and art are our natural expression of this sense of being in love again.

Not only that, it is poetry's fate to be so oriented. Poetry and art cannot help but respond to awe. It is natural and organic for them to do so. They cannot resist. And the more bleak history becomes, the more we need to fall in love, the more we need awe.

EDUCATING FOR AWE

Awe leads to something more than mere knowledge. It leads to wisdom itself. "Awe is the beginning of wisdom," declares Rabbi Heschel. Awe is far more interesting than information. Awe opens the door in our souls, in our hearts and minds. Awe is bigger than we are – like the sacred is bigger than we are – and so it pulls us out of ourselves, it touches on transcendence. It elicits memorable experiences. Awe awakens reverence, respect, and gratitude. How important is gratitude?

Heschel says, "Humanity will destroy itself not from lack of information but from lack of appreciation." That is how important gratitude is: appreciation is life-saving. Its opposite, taking for granted, is life-threatening. Even species threatening. So awe is important. It is part of our survival package.

Healthy knowledge can easily lead to awe. But knowledge that is focused almost exclusively on control is not healthy and it does not lead to awe. It puts awe aside; it even puts awe off. It is off-putting and awe-off-putting. There has been very little room for awe in the classrooms of the modern age. The result is that many youth try to escape education at the earliest possible moment. Education becomes a trial and a burden rather than an occasion for expansion and wonder. Education loses its joy. It becomes less than human. It is a job, not work.

Healthy education will put awe first. When humans care about awe, great things can happen. The mind opens up, and the heart, and, one might say, the soul. Expansion occurs. Wonder returns. The child is kept alive and eager throughout his or her life. Learning becomes a daily event. Books are not put on bookshelves and television does not take over one's psyche.

Indeed, our minds are made for awe. They respond altogether spontaneously to awe. They remember awe. Even on our deathbeds – especially on our deathbeds – do we remember awe.

Awe is an attitude of not taking for granted. When I lost my legs due to polio when I was 12 and a year later got their use back, I was awestruck. I resolved never to take my legs for granted again. If you choke on something and can't breathe, just being able to breathe again is an awesome experience.

The things we have the right to feel most awestruck about are daily things. Food. Where does it come from? It is all sunlight. And drink, too. All drinks are sunlight. Our bodies. They are sunlight. Every organ of our bodies from gallbladder to lungs, from spleen to liver, from heart to brain, from skin to ear, from genitals to intestines, has its story, its history, its awesome gift to reveal. "Is-ness" is a miracle; it is a grace, an awesome gift. We dare not take it for granted or teach the young to take it for granted. We need to teach not just the facts of our bodies and of our lives, but also the wonder and the awe of them.

To pass on this important and fundamental teaching we need adults who admit awe into their consciousness and their stories and their science. Adults who are not only reciters of facts (tape machines can do that for us), but who are *livers of awe*, of what Heschel called "radical amazement." Radical amazement lies at the base of all education, all learning, all wisdom. "Awe is the beginning of wisdom" after all. Not facts, but awe! Yet facts can elicit awe. And they ought to.

How do we bring awe back? We will explore that critical question in greater depth when we speak of education below.

Awful evil: The shadow side of awe

Evil, too, has something to do with awe. In English we use the word "awful" for that which affects us very negatively. Awe is so marvellous that the shadow it extends is itself monstrous and huge. To forfeit awe is to forfeit one's soul, one's life energy, one's powers for love and living. When we forfeit awe, immense becomes our shadow; immense becomes our greed, our violence, our hatred, our hoarding, our forgetting, our not caring. We become that shadow and painful history because we have no medicine to apply to the pain and negative powers. In place of falling in love with the world, we fall into history's shadow sadness. Only our sorrow becomes immense. The rest of us stays very tidy and very small and very controlled.

Rabbi Heschel warned us what happens when we fail to learn awe or to teach awe, when facts alone occupy our classrooms or our minds and hearts. He said, "Forfeit your sense of awe and the universe becomes a marketplace for you." When awe goes out the window, commercialism moves in. Everything has its price. Reductionism reigns. Numbers alone create a (pseudo) awe. We sell our souls for numbers; for more power, money, things, finite relationships. Cosmology, the universe, instead of being approached for its wonders, becomes nothing but a place of buying and selling. Everything has its price, and buying and hawking becomes the only real occupation we feel called to.

The social consequences of this are rampant, as Becker warns us when he talks about the fetish of consumerism in today's society. "We know that when freedom is equated with the right to buy and sell goods it fosters a nation of sheep under the control of the mass media."[9] Lacking a cosmology, we fall into the trap of the world as mall. Thus true freedom must move us beyond today's version of market capitalism wherein, for example, two-thirds of the American economy is based on buying things. (How many of these things are needed?) We are capable, as economist David Korten has proposed, of creating "an economics that works for all" – including generations yet to be born, and societies other than our own, and beings other than just human beings. If we are too lazy to do so we will all pay an awful price.

If we don't put our efforts into creating a healthy economy, Korten warns, then we are acquiescing to a "predatory financial system driven by the single imperative of making ever more money for those who already have lots of it." In short, we are participating in a "war of money against life," a "money pathology" that confuses wealth with money and that makes addicts of us. True wealth "is something that has real value in meeting our needs and fulfilling our wants."[10]

When awe is killed or neglected, we are capable of anything. Hope dies and despair takes over. We lose interest in preserving either our own goodness or anyone else's goodness. We grow indifferent and callous, responding only to the noise of the marketplace and the enticements of commercial numbers. We become prey to an infinite number of options to buy things. We fall out of the real universe and into a man-made perverse universe, a cosmos of consumerism, an ever-expanding shopping mall that goes on infinitely. Until we drop. We shop until we drop. And another life is wasted. Love is missed. Regret reigns. Fear takes over. Flight from death rules the day.

Education has to confront evil. We need to study evil and remember evil and teach about evil, our capacities for it and ways beyond it. Evil is itself awesome in its scope and cruelty. Evil is not "out there" somewhere. It is potentially within us all. Any one of us can be a receptor for evil and an instrument for evil.

Becker proposes a curriculum that is essentially based on our experience of evil and on our response to it, because evil is based on alienation. Specifically, he cites three areas for concentration: First, the history of alienation in one's own life: how evil arises as a result of the law of individual development. Second, the history of alienation in society: how evil arises as a result of the workings of society, and of the evolution of society in history. Third, the problem of alienation under the conditions of existence: how evil arises as a result of the conditions of life itself.[11] Becker defines evil as "whatever encourages group solidarity at the expense of other groups, whatever furthers prejudice and discrimination, nationalism, racism, and so on."[12]

Paulo Freire, in his *Pedagogy of the Oppressed*, also begins education with our experience of evil, oppression, and alienation, and sees true education as that which forges a path to liberation.[13]

We need to study oppression and greed and racism and violence and hoarding and the cold, uncaring heart, if we are to learn anything about liberation or generosity or non-violence or sharing or compassion. It is often wise to first study the opposite of what we want to learn. Then we appreciate it more when we arrive where we want to go, for we have tasted its opposite. Furthermore, evil is often what we have been most exposed to; it is our neighbour; it is near at hand and familiar. Why not look it in the eye and thereby let it lead us to the other side? How will we arrive at the other side without first looking evil in the eye, considering its dimensions and appeals and power?

EDUCATION: FRIEND OR FOE OF EVIL?

Recently, the world commemorated the 60th anniversary of the liberation of Auschwitz, the notorious killing place of children, women, and men whose crime was that they were Jewish (or socialist or homosexual or handicapped). One of the commanders of the Soviet army unit that liberated Auschwitz, Naum Reznik, who had four years of harrowing combat experience previous to seeing the death camp, said that walking into Auschwitz was like entering the gates of hell. Acrid ashes of human flesh floated in the air like waxy snowflakes. Skeletal prisoners greeted him with hollow stares. Piles of human bones, of hair, of eyeglasses, of clothing, were everywhere. Today he says this: "We believed the Germans were an educated nation. We couldn't believe they were capable of bringing about this suffering."[14]

The Germans *were* educated! Educated people are more than capable of bringing about loads of suffering. That is the point. Knowledge alone is power. It needs to be trained and steered to do good and not evil.

This is the lesson to be learned from the horrors of human history. Being educated – alas! – does not mean you won't ever participate in evil. In fact, it means you can participate more efficiently and more effectively and create more rationalisms and excuses for so doing. It was educated chemists who came up with the exact formulas for the gassing of 1.2 million humans at Auschwitz.

This is why only wisdom can save us. Knowing science and having knowledge gives power; it does not tell us how to use power humanely. We are, all of us – and the educated especially – capable of bringing about untold amounts of suffering. Plato long ago told us this truth when he said that "without the knowledge of good and evil the use and excellence of [all the sciences] will be found to have failed us."

Reznik's words remind me of an observation by a prophet of our time, Thomas Berry, who warns us that "most of the destruction of the planet today is happening at the hands of people with PhDs." Is this not a wake-up call for all educators? All teachers? All politicians wanting to spend tax dollars for education? All citizens? All parents and all students?

For we are embarked today, as a species, on paths that will make the Holocaust appear to be a minor tragedy. The extinction of life forms taking place today is the largest since 65 million years ago. The implications of a warming climate for raising food and feeding humanity; its role in wiping out villages and cities along seacoasts, as well as species of plants, animals, trees, fishes; in altering weather patterns and increasing the frequency of hurricanes – all these things are already affecting our lives profoundly and more bad news will be forthcoming. In relation to the destruction wrought by the tsunami in southeast Asia, scientists have determined that where coral reefs had been destroyed by human enterprises (50 percent of the world's coral reefs have been destroyed), the tsunami did its worst damage. Where coral reefs were intact, the tsunami did much less damage because the reefs themselves absorbed the powerful waves.

The 20th century's atrocities of war (42 million persons killed in the Second World War alone), of nuclear power (Hiroshima and Nagasaki as curtain raisers on this), and of ecological degradation, were not caused by evil forces "out there" or "abroad somewhere." These happened and are happening at the hands and minds of university graduates and our university intelligentsia. The 20th century accomplished mass slaughters of our species – 90 million killed in military conflict and another 80 million killed in social pogroms by Hitler, Stalin, Mao, and others. Zbigniew Brzezinski calls this the "politics of organized insanity." These numbers are, as Brzezinski observes, "more than the total killed in all previous wars, civil conflicts, and religious persecutions throughout human history."[15] Friedrich Nietzsche, as James Garrison points out, intuited a century earlier that human rationality was heading towards "an orgy of violence."[16] We have passed through that orgy. What now? What is education's role in all this?

It is time for some morality. For some choices. For some wisdom. It takes ethics and morality to use power humanely. It takes wisdom to curb knowledge, to steer it for the greater good, to turn the lead of power (knowledge) into the gold of wisdom.

Awe and wisdom

Awe is the door to wisdom. "Awe is the beginning of wisdom," says the ancient proverb. This is one more reason why a newly renewed education must begin with a sense and practice of awe. For all courses and all topics, we need to begin with awe. What is the awe in being a lawyer? A writer? A ball player? A teacher? A doctor? A business person? A therapist? A welder? A carpenter? A taxi cab driver? A human being? Where is the awe in your life and in your work? In your religion and in your citizenship?

Wisdom, as we shall see below, is the direction in which education must now escort us. If our species cannot move from knowledge to wisdom, we are doomed. Wisdom can save us. Our times call for wisdom and not just knowledge. All avenues to wisdom need to be explored and even exploited. Awe is such an avenue, such a path, such a way. The way of wisdom. That is our destiny and our salvation. Education needs to be part of the solution, not part of the problem. Education needs to flush wisdom out from its hidden places, where it has been shyly and demurely holding back during the modern era's rush to knowledge, facts, and power trips.

The journey to wisdom begins with awe. Awe so engages the right hemisphere of the brain – and the heart as well – that rationalisms and left-brain-itis cannot dominate any longer. Awe floods our souls, flushes our minds, and waters our hearts. There is no medicine against awe. There is no blocking wisdom.

3·

A: ANCESTOR-BASED

Now we will break down the word AWE. First comes the letter A. A stands for ancestors. An authentic education today must honour the ancestors.

The ancestors are listening and watching, listening to what is going on and what is not going on. Watching our education and our miseducation; what we are teaching our young and what we are failing to teach them; our choices that are life giving or biophiliac, and our choices that are death-dealing and necrophiliac. The ancestors are with us hoping to guide us, encourage us, give us direction and support. They know we need help, that we are ignorant. And they know how dangerous we have become, with so much knowledge and so little wisdom.

Recovering ancestor awareness

Who are our ancestors and how are they feeling about us?

A telling account was given in the recent tragedy of the coal miners lost in a West Virginia coal mine. One of the miners, Martin Toler Jr., left a message behind as he knew that he was dying. Written in block letters with an ink pen on a scrap of paper, it said, "Tell all I see them on the other side… It wasn't bad. I just went to sleep. I love you."

These are moving and honest words coming from an ordinary yet courageous person among us. First, he wants to say, as his final words, "I love you." He further expresses that love by assuring his loved ones that his death was not painful. And he also testifies to expecting to reunite "on the other side." There is no hint of self-pity. This concrete testimony to the power of love tells us volumes about our ancestors, that is, those who have gone to the other side. They *do* care about us; we *are* in their final thoughts, just as our loved ones will be in our final thoughts. And all they leave us, their love and memories, are now ours to keep and to use (or of course to forget and to misuse). Once again the power of memory rises to the surface. Do we remember the ancestors? We can be sure they remember us.

Ancestors care. In doing so, they give us strength to continue and to carry on the fullness of life, the history of love. They support us.

Who is an ancestor? Etymologically, the word comes from the Latin for *antecedere,* "to go before." Our ancestors are those who have gone before us and that is a great many. We stand on their shoulders; we inherit their genes, their ways, their lessons learned, their teachings, their stories, their mistakes. Ancestors are antecedents or forebears – which means those who have been before.

In the modern era, driven as it was by the myth that we were constantly making progress just because we were gathering more and more knowledge, we were taught to always look forward, to look ahead, to dream ahead of better and better times. We were taught, verbally and non-verbally, to ignore the past, to ridicule the pre-modern peoples, to hold the medieval world in disdain (confusing the Middle Ages with the "Dark Ages"), to believe that the Native American, African, Pacific Island peoples that Europeans "discovered" (i.e., ran into) in the late 15th century were in every way and every respect inferior to the great Western and white race, religion, and "civilization."

One of the hottest theological arguments of that day (comparable to today's religious arguments against homosexuality for homosexual people) was the following: Do Indians, the native people of the Americas, have souls? It took a dogged Dominican friar and missionary, Bartalomew de las Casas, special trips back to Spain from South America to debate theologians formally about the reality that, Yes! Indians do have souls.

In fact, las Casas concluded that not only do Indians have souls, but their civilization was superior to European civilization, and that even if there was some blood spilled for certain sacrificial ritual ceremonies in their tradition, still, they did not indulge in the sacrificial slaughter of humans that Western war-making accomplished in his day. Imagine what las Casas would say today after the Holocaust, after the two world wars, after Nagasaki and Hiroshima, and during the current planetary extinction of so many species and so many indigenous tribes, *still* and *all* in the name of "progress," meaning capitalism's advancement. "The marketplace made me do it" – that is the mantra of so much degradation and enslavement of peoples for the past 500 years – just as Heschel declares happens whenever awe is neglected.

The Western word that comes closest to that of *ancestor* is probably *tradition*. (I prefer the term ancestor because it is more personal.) Fierce wars have been waged over traditions all around the globe. The Sunni and the Shiites are engaged in such a polemic in our time; orthodox, conservative, and reformed Jews; Protestant and Roman Catholic, opus dei Catholic and liberation theology Catholic, Lutheran Protestant or Presbyterian Protestant, Orthodox and Anglican, Dominicans and Franciscans, all claim their particular traditions or interpretations of their ancestors, and even interpretations of interpretations. Which traditions, which teachings of the ancestors, are most valuable and most worth keeping? That is a question as we try to simplify our lives and even our education at this time in history.

One of the tasks of elders is to pass on traditions, to pass on stories and the teachings of the ancestors, and to make wise decisions about which stories are most needed at certain points in time. For elders to emerge to do their important task, they themselves must know the traditions, know the ancestors. It is scary when you encounter in our day some of the silly and dangerous notions that people, who claim to know the ancestors, propound when they in fact have not done their inner work or their intellectual work and do not know their own ancestral heritage. This is true of politicians who do not know the constitution of the United States, as well as of people who call themselves Christians but do not know their tradition in any of its diversity and richness.

I recently encountered a Southern Baptist minister who told me that in his tradition a minister does not have to attend school and that he never studied to this day any of the 1900 years of Christian theology. "We only studied the Bible," he confessed. But he did not study the languages in which the Bible was written, so it might be more accurate to say that he *projected* on the Bible. How sad it was to listen to a preacher who knew nothing of the efforts of other Christians through the ages to interpret the Bible and to wrestle with its issues.

There are people today who call themselves Christians who in fact are teaching not the love, justice, and compassion that Jesus taught, but are eager to divide people, Us against

Them; to destroy the environment; and to bring about a new apocalypse. Certain Muslims distort the Islamic tradition as teaching hatred of people of other faiths. Distortions in tradition can produce crackpots and loony bin believers. That is how powerful ignorance is. That is why education is so important in crisis times.

LESSONS FROM THE ANCESTORS

Honouring and respecting those who have gone before does not come easily to the modern mindset. But to postmodern consciousness our ancestral awareness can be a kind of salvation. One reason for this is that, in many respects, our ancestors represent the shadow side, the neglected or repressed side of our own selves. True self-knowledge includes awareness of our hidden and neglected sides. It is not that we pine to, or even could if we wanted to, return to the past and live there.

We are postmodern. All of us, even indigenous peoples. We have passed through a time as a species that cannot be undone. We cannot turn back; it is too late for that. And besides, not everything we learned in the modern era was negative by any means. What we *can* do is reconnect our lost selves, those parts of ourselves that were cut off or forgotten or buried by the heavy agendas of the modern period. We do this by paying attention to our ancestors and how they lived on this earth, how they educated their young and themselves, the important questions they set for their young and the pedagogy by which they did so.

THE COSMOS AS ANCESTOR

But our ancestors are not just the two-legged ones. Now that today's science is helping us to relearn the ancient principle of interconnectivity, we are continually made aware that we humans and all our human ancestors owe our existence to rocks and waters, to forests and soil, to plants and animals, to oxygen and carbon, to sun and moon, to tides and photosynthesis, to the solar system itself and to the supernovas and the galaxies and the atoms and the original fireball. All are kin. All are of the same stuff, the same kind, all are connected. And all are our ancestors.

But this current teaching is also very ancient. Indigenous peoples and pre-modern peoples thrived on it. The most important questions indigenous peoples put forward to their young were these: How did it all begin? What is creation? What is our home? Where does it all come from, how are we part of it, and where are we going – or where ought we to be going – and how do we get there? This is what life is about; this is what ethics and morality are about. They are about our place in the universe and the universe's place in us. This is our context. All else is a response to this context.

Eddie Kneebone is an Aboriginal from Australia. In an interview, he talks about what matters to his people, who may constitute the oldest extant tribe of people on the earth. He says that he has come to realize, living in Western culture as he does, "that man created the building that he calls churches, God created the world. If I look for God then it will be in the environment that he built." And what is key to that environment?

In the daytime, we see the particulars – "trees, birds, rivers, the wind in the clouds, and the sunshine. This is the environment that is revealed during the daylight hours, that we take for granted." But at night another world comes alive and is revealed to us – this is the world of the universe itself. "Every clear night we can look up and see millions of stars. That is also a part of our lives." But when Aboriginals look up at night they do not only see stars: "They never saw stars. They only saw the campfires of their ancestors on their journey. The bright stars were the ancestors who were not long gone; the dimmer stars were the ancestors further on the journey."[1] The ancestors are busy sitting around their campfires looking back to see the campfires of the living ones on earth. "The Aboriginals looked up and really believed that their eyes could meet."

Do we believe this? Can our eyes meet our ancestors? Can we connect with them also and without shame or apology?

Notice how, in this ancient teaching, the cosmos itself is an ancestor. And how, in today's creation story from science, we learn this ancient teaching again – so much so that we might say that "cosmology" is another word for "ancestor." For the cosmos has gone before; it is a forerunner, an antecedent, a parent, a cousin, our ancient kin. The cosmos is all time and all space and all beings that have brought us thus far to this time and this space. To quote Eddie Kneebone again, "All objects are living and share the same soul or spirit that Aboriginals share. Therefore all Aboriginals have a kinship with the environment. The soul or spirit is common – only the shape is different, but no less important."[2]

This same spirit of kinship with all being is exalted by Howard Thurman, who comes from the African and African American tradition. "As a child, the boundaries of my life spilled over into the mystery of the ocean and the wonder of the dark nights and the wooing of the wind until the breath of Nature and my own breath seemed to be one – it was resonant to the tonality of God..." Notice the role of awe and wonder in this ancient practice of finding oneself within nature's profound embrace.

Thurman continues:

There is magic all around us – in the rocks, the trees, and the minds of men... and he who strikes the rock aright may find them where he will... We are so overwhelmed by the personal but vast impact of the particularity of living objects that we are scarcely aware of a much more profound fact in our midst, and that is that life itself is alive.[3]

Yes, life itself is alive! In the Middle Ages, the Christian mystic and activist Hildegard of Bingen wrote of similar experiences when she sings, "I, the fiery life of divine wisdom, I ignite the beauty of the plains, I sparkle the waters, I burn in the sun, and the moon, and the stars. With wisdom I order all rightly, above all I determine truth." And again, "Invisible life that sustain all, I awaken to life everything in every waft of air. The air is life, greening and blooming. The waters flow with life. The sun is lit with life. The moon, when waning, is again rekindled by the sun, waxing with life once more. The stars shine, radiating with life-light." And sounding like a postmodern physicist she declared, "Everything that is in the heavens, on the earth, and under the earth, is penetrated with connectedness, is penetrated with relatedness."[4]

It is basic spiritual practice and courtesy in the ancient cultures of the world, be they African, Asian, or Indigenous, to honour the ancestors, to thank them, to call them in whenever we gather, to receive their gifts with an open and generous heart, to follow their ways as we know them and can adapt them to our own times. In short, to remember and honour our relationship with the ancestors. This putting of relationship at the centre of our activities again amounts to a veritable revolution in our time, because the modern era was not about honouring the ancestors. It was about conquering the earth and overcoming those peoples who still honoured their ancestors. Such people were put down as "pagans" who "worship their ancestors." They did not worship their ancestors; they honoured them. They *re-membered* them, making them members again of the larger community and of the current community.

When Einstein began to unravel the certitudes and mechanical thinking of the modern era by his theory of relativity, he may have been setting the stage for what we can call today, 100 years after he published his paper on relativity, a theory of relationship with the ancestors. Our ancestors, be they stars or atoms, galaxies or rocks, carbon, oxygen, hydrogen, or helium, fishes or primates, or sun or moon, grandparents or great-grandparents, aunts or uncles, must be smiling upon us as we wake up anew to their gifts and the inheritance they have left us. An inheritance of the beauty and health, the wonder and joy, the work and responsibilities of being humans on this earth and in this greater home of the universe itself. Remembering is a holy act, a healing act, a salvific act.

OUR MANY ANCESTORS

We all have ancestors. Everyone with a belly button has ancestors. But often we do not know our ancestors, we are out of touch with them, we have cut ourselves off from them or have forgotten them. A time of uprooting like ours is also a time of re-rooting, of knowing our ancestors and knowing them so well that we can distinguish their wisdom from their habits, what is important from what is not important.

It is knowing what to take along with us and what to leave behind. And knowing how to blend the wisdom of the past with the needs of the present.

We all have ancestors and we do not have just a few ancestors. Our ancestors are not just the literal members of our family tree – though they are that. Our ancestors include members of our cultural tree and our religious tree and our ethnic tree, our professional trees, gender tree, gender preference tree.

For example, Christians have Christian ancestors – the saints, the prophets, the martyrs and theologians, the sinners and mystics, the founders and reformers – all these from Jesus to Paul, from Hildegard to Aquinas, from Francis to Meister Eckhart, from Dorothy Day to Teilhard de Chardin, from Martin Luther to Martin Luther King Jr., from Pope John XXIII to Florence Nightingale, from Julian of Norwich to Iranaeus – all these can rightly be called "ancestors" if one is a Christian.

The same holds for members of the Jewish faith whose ancestors include Martin Buber and Karl Marx, Rabbi Heschel and Moses Maimonides, Abraham, Sara, David, Moses, Isaiah, Ezekiel, and many more.

Buddhists have their ancestors. Muslims theirs. Native Americans theirs. Africans and Celts, theirs.

In addition, professions boast their own ancestors. Billie Holiday and Louis Armstrong in jazz; Frank Lloyd Wright, Julia Morgan, and Edward Sullivan in architecture; Mozart,

Bach, Beethoven, and Hildegard in music; Galileo, Copernicus, Newton, Einstein, and Darwin in science; etc.

Ethnic histories boast their ancestors: Howard Thurman and Marcus Garvey, Sojourner Truth, Malcolm X, and Harriet Tubman among others if you are black; Cesar Chavez or Simon Bolivar if you are Latino; Black Elk and Chief Seattle and many more if you are Native American.

And nations boast their ancestors. In the United States we sing of the exploits of George Washington and Thomas Jefferson, of Benjamin Franklin and Abraham Lincoln, of Franklin Delano Roosevelt and John Fitzgerald Kennedy. In other countries there are other leaders to boast of.

Getting to know our ancestors can be a lifelong task. It can keep one young and alive discovering and rediscovering one's ancestors. As a sociologist has written, in these postmodern times we all belong to many communities. We are not just our ethnic or religious ancestors, but also our professional and national ancestors.

Ourselves as ancestors

Some day, long after we our gone, we ourselves will be remembered as ancestors. We will be questioned about the wisdom of our choices and how we did or did not choose wisdom or pass wisdom on during our lifetimes. Acknowledging that moment in the future ought to inspire us to care deeply about everything we call education in our lifetime. It ought to pique our curiosity about learning, which so much informs our ethical and moral decision making.

How well are we doing at acknowledging, remembering, and even thanking our ancestors, and at carrying on the best of their work? That is a basic issue in education: ancestral remembrance, remembering what our ancestors held dear and necessary for survival. What skills, what practices, what behaviours did they countenance for our survival? And not just for our survival, but also for our joy? Our ancestors did not just struggle to survive, they also struggled to find meaning and to share joy in family and tribe, among all earthlings and among different tribes. Of course, they failed at this at times just as we do. But their struggle for harmony and balance, justice and celebration, and therefore for compassion, is as real for us today as it was for them eons ago.

Science calls this quest for balance, which is found in all eco-systems as well as in all bodies, homeostasis. Homeostasis is another name for justice. Without it, things fall apart permanently. Without it, life cannot endure. Societies, too, fall apart without homeostasis or justice. Species can destroy themselves from lack of justice. Especially a species as generously endowed with intelligence and creativity, as well as powers of destruction, as is the human species.

Are we studying our ancestors? Are we learning what they have to teach us today? How can we do a better job of learning their lessons? Surely learning their language is very important. And their ceremonies. And their worldviews, the way they saw the world, the stars, the relationships between humans and other creatures, between humans and other humans.

But that is not enough. We also need to search into their wisdom, their love of wisdom, the understanding of what wisdom entails. The traditional name for this search is philosophy, or love of wisdom. Unfortunately, the modern era practically destroyed the meaning of philosophy for subsequent generations just as it destroyed the term university. Instead of being a place to find one's place in the universe, which was the original meaning of the university when it was invented in the 12th century, university has come to mean a place to become specialized in your own specific profession. With no sense of the whole, the university is kept together only by the glue of competition and budget-making. Money has become its glue more than wisdom.

When that is the case, when parts prevail over the whole, ethics is essentially lost and rarely taught. For ethics concerns the whole; it is ultimately about our relationship to one another as a whole, as well as individuals; and the "one another" includes not just our nearest relatives or neighbours or even members of our species, but all our relations. Ethics concerns all our relations. Our relations to ancestors, but also to those not yet born, those seven generations from today. How will they judge our actions? How will they see our wars and our budgets for war making versus our budgets to relieve poverty?

Our huge unsustainable gulfs between haves and have-nots? Between rich and poor? Between those without food and work and shelter and health care, and those with too much of everything? How will they view our stockpiles of nuclear weapons and of nuclear waste, and our nuclear manufacturing of still more unprocessable wastes?

ANCESTRAL AWE

When we look to understand the recent history of our species, with special attention focused on our passage from pre-modern to modern (1492: the printing press and Columbus' invasion of the Americas), and modern to postmodern (1960s), we find it important to lay out some basic differences between the various worldviews involved.

One difference is the approach to awe. Pre-moderns had it. They had awe. They were at home with awe. Consider the examples above from Howard Thurman, Eddie Kneebone, and Hildegard of Bingen. Consider, for example, how Thomas Aquinas in the 13th century said that both poetry and philosophy begin at the same point: with wonder and awe.

In contrast, in the modern era, Descartes said that philosophy begins with doubt or skepticism. Those are very different starting points indeed. The modern era practically lost awe. It did not want to confess that there was something bigger than humanity that could inspire us or inspire awe. All was subjected to the human agenda. We thought we could know everything in order to control it. That was the agenda: control.

Humans do not just participate in awe; we also make awe. Our stories, our lives, our art and music, our theatre and films, our struggles for justice – all these are stories of awe that we leave behind us. Human creativity introduces even more awe into the universe.

Consider how profound the experience of awe is when we listen to the real story of our forefathers, foremothers, and forerunners. Their stories move us and motivate us. No matter who are ancestors are. Are you an African American? Then the awe of your ancestors, who came against their will to this country but struggled to survive slavery and breaking up of families and being robbed of their religion and their land and their greater, extended, family – what is more awesome than that?

Yet there is also awe in their pre-slavery story. The village life. The wisdom learned from tens of thousands of years of living, begetting babies and raising them, gardening, hunting, learning, teaching, ritual-making, being elders. The awe of survival in the jungles of Africa with the animals, with the insects, the heat, the storms, the wild – all stories of awe. And what about the original humans who were from Africa? How about that awesome story – the very first human tribe, the ones who discovered fire, who dared to move on to new territories, the curiosity of that, their courage, their imaginations. And what about the amazing Egyptian civilization, which is truly, in so many ways, the mother of all civilization – the place where Pythagoras studied math for 14 years and where Homer studied and learned for eight years, the place where astronomy was so profoundly learned that pyramids could be constructed just right…

There is awe in all these stories and in studying one's ancestors one is struck by awe. Their powerful works awaken awe in us, and with that gratitude and understanding.

Are you an Asian American? What about the stories of your ancestors, ones who came to America in the 19th century and who, against all odds, survived on the railroad building lines. These people, who had their religion and cultural ways taken away from them, who were forbidden to bring wives with them, who endured pogroms and lynchings, who were not allowed to vote until the 1940s; it's amazing what they accomplished and what they endured. Awesome stories to tell there also.

And what about Irish and Celtic Americans?

And other European tribes, the Italians and Polish, the Armenians and the Jews, and many others?

And Latino Americans?

What we learn when we explore our ancestral stories is that there is no shortage of awe. The amazing story of human survival even in the most dire of times – that is what catches our hearts and minds. That is what produces "radical amazement."

We experience great awe not just from exposure to our human ancestors, but from exposure to our non-human ones as well. Creation stories fill us with awe. Our contemporary creation story does exactly that. When we learn that hydrogen atoms comprise 60 percent of our body and that they are 13 billion years old – that is awesome. When you look in the mirror and really know that you are looking at 14 billion years of history – that is awesome. It fires one up to live fully and to live hard and to live justly. And to educate with passion and respect for our awe-bearing species. Or it should.

Yes, there is awe everywhere – provided we are on the lookout for it. Our ancestors expect us to honour awe. And the wisdom it brings with it.

4.

W: Wisdom-Based

The W in A.W.E. can stand for wisdom. Our education needs to be focused on wisdom and not on mere knowledge.

Now that we have talked of awe and also of our ancestors, we have created a context for discussing wisdom. We must awaken to awe before we can discuss wisdom, for "Awe is the beginning of wisdom." We must also talk of ancestors before we talk of wisdom. This is so not just because pre-modern people tried very hard to put wisdom before knowledge, but also because connecting to our ancestors takes us to wisdom's gate just as the *Tao Te Ching* declares: "Just realize where you come from: this is the essence of wisdom." To know our origins and remember our many ancestors is to enter the portals of wisdom.

Knowledge vs. wisdom

and the corruption of philosophy

The sad and sorry truth is that wisdom has not been on the educational agenda in Western cultures for centuries. The modern era put wisdom on the shelf and put all its eggs into the knowledge basket. We actually ran from and distorted the very meaning of the word *philosophy,* which etymologically means "love of wisdom," but which has come to mean less a love of wisdom or a study of wisdom than a study of human knowledge and modern science, often divorced from ethical implications. One current scholar, Peter Kingsley, says this about philosophy in the modern era: "Centuries have been spent destroying the truth about what [philosophy] once was. We only have eyes now for what philosophy has become – no idea of what it no longer is."

We have invented computers to store all our data and detailed information. But what inventions exist to store and liven our wisdom? Kingsley comments:

> The basic meaning of philosophy is love of wisdom. That means very little anymore. We have plenty of room in our lives for knowledge and data, for learning and information, amusement and entertainment; but not for wisdom... Instead of the love of wisdom philosophy turned itself into the love of talking and arguing about the love of wisdom.[1]

Philosophy became a study of certain philosophical theories but had very little to do with discerning wisdom for living life fully, deeply, and honourably. Philosophy was no longer about living wisely but about thinking in sophisticated language. Kingsley says, "we create schemes and structures, and climb up and down inside them. But these are just monkey tricks and parlour games to console us and distract us from the longing in our hearts."[2] It is that longing in the heart that abstract philosophical games in no way address. Philosophy became relegated to adults – and generally to esoterically talking adults. It was a rare thing if a philosopher could communicate with youth or even with people outside his or her own esoteric discipline. Children's wisdom was seldom inquired after.

The pursuit of knowledge in the modern era uncovered much that is useful for living, including electricity and flushing toilets, sewer systems and bridges that span great distances, trips to the moon and back, medicine and surgery and drugs that can relieve suffering and prolong life, intelligent guesses that predict catastrophes such as hurricanes and volcanoes, thereby saving lives. Much of the modern era's findings are good and useful.

But how much is wise? How much wisdom has been uncovered and passed on, that is taught, in our educational establishments, in the modern era? And does any of this translate into postmodern educational needs?

Knowledge without wisdom is dangerous. Knowledge by itself is raw power. With knowledge we can "bomb them back to the stone age," as one general put it in his zeal to win the Vietnam War. But only wisdom tells us to find other means than winning at all costs and obliterating our existence and our souls in the process.

There is a Celtic saying that warns, "Never give a loaded gun to a young man who has not first learned to dance." Who are we to take life if we have not first learned to love life? So, too, education is a kind of loaded gun, a weapon. It should not be thrust into the hands of people who have not first learned to dance, that is, to love and celebrate life.

The time has come for wisdom schools

The modern era, which gave us industrial civilization, has pretty much reduced education to knowledge factories. And very conservative ones at that, as the Mills college president we cited earlier testifies. What we need today is not more knowledge factories but wisdom schools.

A wisdom school is concerned not just with certain topics or content. It is also concerned about method, about form and pedagogy therefore. The greatest revolutions in education come about when pedagogy changes, for pedagogy is the form in which we do education. Education is not itself transformed until pedagogy is transformed. I will give two examples from history.

The first is a little known event that happened in New England in the 17th century. It was decided that a number of Indian children and white children would exchange classrooms. Indian kids would go to school in the "little red school house" while white kids would follow the Native elders out into the woods. The experiment was to last six weeks.

After just a few weeks, all the Indian kids ran away from the schoolhouse and returned to their tribe. When the six weeks were up, the white kids did not return to their households or to the little red schoolhouse. Nor after the seventh week. Their parents went hunting for them and when they found them the children simply made clear that they were happier learning in nature and outside the schoolroom in the Indian fashion than they were in the white way of learning.

This is a story about pedagogy and form. It is about diverse ways of learning.

There are many ways of learning; as a species we have from the get-go taken it upon ourselves to teach our offspring. But there is no one way, no one form, no one pedagogy for doing so. I believe that it is more our forms and ways and pedagogies that are obstructing learning today and rendering it less fun than it should be, than it is lack of money or good teachers or sound unions or enlightened overseers. If we change the form, new energy and new teachers and leaders with educational imagination will show up. With that enthusiasm will flow money and support.

A second historic example of a revolution in pedagogy occurred at the level of adult education in the 12th and early 13th centuries. For 800 years, education had been pretty much in the hands of monastic schools run by monks. These monks did a good job during a very cold and dark period in European history. They created texts and libraries to house the teachings of old and they dedicated themselves to teaching the young, especially those of the noble and knightly classes. But their main pedagogy was one of citing authorities. "Because Augustine (or Gregory or some other 'father') said it," became the bottom line on what was true and not true. Theology became a matter of citing authorities.

Then came a revolution. It came from Islam. It came from what today we call Iraq and Iran, that is, from Persia. And it came via Spain, where Islamic culture was alive and flourishing. This revolutionary pedagogy was called scholasticism. It was revolutionary because it displaced a pedagogy of citing authorities with a pedagogy of asking questions. Scholasticism in its heyday was all about asking questions. The best answers, the most convincing answers, were given more weight than were citations from authorities. Logic was more important than pedigree. Carl Jung and other notable thinkers have commented on how scholasticism ushered in the methodology of modern science, which is also about asking questions and finding verifiable answers.

Along with scholasticism, the entire educational enterprise moved from the rural and feudal-based domain of monastic control into the city. There universities were born, beginning in Paris (my alma mater). There questions ruled more than the citing of authorities. There the inquiring mind was encouraged. Thomas Aquinas, very much a part of that educational revolution, taught that authority is the least weighty argument one can find.

Eventually, as we all know too well, scholasticism became corrupt – the questions became routine or silly and irrelevant, and the answers uninspired. One might say that scholasticism was co-opted by the powers of state and church. But for about 100 years previous to this co-optation, the introduction of this revolutionary pedagogy stirred the hearts and minds of the young and of several generations. It launched a revolution in education – the movement from the monastic educational system in the countrysides to the newly invented universities in all the great cities of Europe. And it sowed the seeds for future science and future education.

These two examples underscore the importance of pedagogy and the forms that we choose or do not choose to educate with. Ever since the 18th century, when Francis Bacon said that he would replace form with law (meaning the mechanical law of the 18th-century notion that the universe is a machine like a clock is a machine), we have underestimated the power of form and our responsibility to consciously choose forms in a deliberate way. We have imagined that form is absolute and immutable, that form is like a machine – something not to be tinkered with. Thus we fail to think enough of form in education; we think the problems in education are about content alone. "More math classes! More computer classes! More exams!" we shout. Or we imagine the issues are about personalities: new professors, school board members, principals, and presidents. We fail to take responsibility for critiquing and reinventing *forms* of learning.

The real crisis in education is a crisis in form. A crisis in pedagogy. The issue is not so much *what* we teach as *how* we teach. One cannot teach wisdom in a form that welcomes only knowledge. One cannot teach wisdom in forms that ignore chakras other than head chakras, forms that ignore the heart, the guts, the feet. Forms that take these things seriously make wisdom possible again.

EDUCATION AND THE DISADVANTAGED

Further evidence of education's failure is that so many young people of colour drop out of school. Studies show that 50 percent of Latino and black youth in the United States will not graduate from high school. In Baltimore today, 76 percent of young black men are not graduating from high school. Does this mean God and nature made these youngsters with less intelligence than others? With less desire to know and learn? Of course not.

Maybe our high schools are not doing their job right – maybe this first postmodern generation has to learn differently than was proposed during the modern era. Maybe we need different kinds of high schools, ones that appeal to the creativity of our youth and prepare them for creative work. Maybe less time at desks and more time in art labs will be the way to elicit the wisdom of youth. Maybe more cosmology, which provides *context* and less *text*, is important. Maybe creativity needs to be a priority. Maybe the pre-modern spirit of indigenous consciousness is more prevalent in youth of colour and they feel as a result less present to and less excited by an almost exclusively modern, European mode of thinking and learning, which is heavily anthropocentric and which values words over images, texts over art.

Rabbi Abraham Heschel warns us of the dangers of adults serving up forms of education that no longer work for many young people when he observes that "termination of education is the beginning of despair."[3] With despair, young people's lives turn downhill very quickly or as Thomas Aquinas puts it, despair is the "most dangerous" of all the sins for when one is in despair one does not care about what happens to oneself and subsequently to others. The stakes are high indeed when forms of education are failing all around us.

In the state of California today, there are more black men in prison than in school. Is there a connection between incarceration and inept education? Are young people thrown into the streets where they must fend for themselves because our educational forms do not seize their minds and imaginations?

At Fremont High School in Los Angeles, two-thirds of the ninth graders drop out before graduation. Eighty percent of the students are from disadvantaged black and Latino families. Poverty, more than any other single factor, dictates school success. Maybe schools in poor neighbourhoods should be different kinds of schools. Dropouts often join gangs and so we can say that miseducation (which is also missed education, an opportunity that is missed) contributes to gang and growing prison populations. "The educational system could be a powerful factor in preventing students from joining gangs," comments one student of inner-city gang culture. "In general the gang subculture is a dropout subculture," observes Tom Hayden, in his fine study on *Street Wars: Gangs and the Future of Violence*.[4] Gang members are very often school dropouts.

But that does not mean gang members are anti-learning. It means only that the educational experience they are exposed to did not work for them. David Brotherton, at the John Jay College of Criminal Justice in Manhattan, has been leading a team doing research with the Latin Kings gang for several years. He stresses the critical role of schools in the inner city and summarizes his interviews with gang members this way:

> ☞ Gang students want to be mentored. They want attention and crave to be valued other than in street gangs.

☞ Gang students have hope. Many see their gang experience as transitional; all speak of wanting to leave at some point.

☞ Gang members are expressive, with a flair for artistic imagery and poetry.

☞ Gang students are very interested in their ethnic culture.

☞ Gang students are communal and collective; they hate the competition and favouritism in typical school culture, but are open to learning together.[5]

There are clues and hints here for how to develop an educational program for gang members and potential gang members. One might call it "prison prevention education" or "gang prevention education." The way follows the dimensions of education we will lay forth in this manifesto. Briefly told, they are as follows:

☞ *Cosmology.* (This teaches the value of the individual loved and birthed by the universe itself.) I once spoke at a retreat for workers in south central LA and I emphasized the new cosmology. I was backed up by Marcel Diallo, a rapper from Oakland who would rap on the spot what I was saying. When we finished, a woman stood up and said, "I have been working in south central LA for 18 years and I do not know any group anywhere who is more interested in cosmology than the young people there."

☞ *Creativity.* Tap into that flair for artistic imagery and poetry. Start with that. (Recently, I met a young man who is dedicated to helping street youth. He began by living in an ashram in New Delhi committed to the street youth there. Now he works in New York City. He tells me that the great gift of imagination and creativity, which street youth possess, is so often over looked by the well-meaning agencies who try to help them. He and his partner have gotten design agencies to hire these young people because of their creative abilities.)

☞ *Ancestral awareness.* Tap into their curiosity about their ethnic heritage, its heroes and struggles and achievements, and its beauty and rituals.

☞ *Compassion.* Tap into the communal, collective, and justice-oriented ethic of this subculture, their commitment to their community. One educator, Belvie Rooks, worked with youth of south central Los Angeles to develop a CD-ROM on the ecological poison found in their neighbourhoods.

In a recent year, New York City spent $8000 per child in its public schools but $93,000 per child in its new South Bronx juvenile detention center. What kind of investment makes sense: $8000 per student in school or $93,000 per youth offender in detention centres?

Teachers in the inner city received salaries of $42,000 per year; those in suburbs received salaries of $82,000 per year. A serious study comparing schools in poor neighbourhoods to those in affluent ones found that the disadvantaged were "12 times more likely to be in a school with untrained, uncredentialed teachers; twice as likely to lack adequate textbooks; and twice as likely to have nonfunctional bathrooms."[6] One school in Los Angeles with 3500 students had only two functioning bathrooms each for boys and girls, and just one college counsellor for the entire student body.

A few years ago, a woman came up to me following a lecture I gave in Ohio and told me this story. She said a judge came to her and complained, "I am sick and tired of sending high school dropouts to jail. Can you create a school I could send them to as an alternative?" She told me she designed a school based on my writings and that it was 100 percent about arts and creativity. From 9:00 in the morning until 4:00 in the afternoon, students studied dance, theatre, poetry, painting, music, rap, and video. What happened? The students showed up. They stayed over and asked faculty to stay over. After a few months, they derived a language through the arts to express their anger and their dreams and their visions. Then they started asking questions about "this Shakespeare dude," or algebra, or history and geography.

Maybe we are doing education backwards. Maybe first we ought to motivate; and then develop a fuller curriculum.

As W. B. Yeats put it, "Education is not about filling a pail but about lighting a fire." First comes the lighting of the fire. "Firement" comes first.

All tribes, all cultures, all peoples have always committed themselves to teaching the young. But what to teach them? And how? And for what agreed-upon purposes?

These are age-old questions and they challenge us today in new and charged ways, as humanity enters what may be a final act in its existence. As more and more humans dwell on the earth, and more and more are young people under 16 years of age, we do indeed face a countdown to our survival as a species. Is education as we practice it part of the problem or part of the solution?

ELEMENTS OF WISDOM

There is a marvellous passage in the Book of Wisdom in the Hebrew Bible that lays out much of what is meant by wisdom. It goes like this:

Simply I learned about Wisdom...
The design of the universe,
The force of its elements
Beginning and end of time,
Changes in the sun's course,
Variation of seasons,
Cycles of years,
Positions of stars,

Natures of animals,
Tempers of beasts,
Powers of winds,
Thoughts of humanity,
Uses of plants,
Virtues of roots.
Such things as are hidden I learned,
For Wisdom,
The Artisan of all,
Taught me. (7:17–22)

Wisdom is herself a teacher; she is "artisan of all." She is all about creativity and art and the aesthetic. She is a revealer, for she unveils secrets and hidden things. One has to deepen oneself for the journey into wisdom. She is not on the surface, but down deep. Underground. In the darkness. Below the light. Not to be found exclusively on the surface or in the daytime.

   She is also simple – "simply I learned about Wisdom." In other places in the wisdom literature of Israel, she is said to "walk the streets." She will be found among the everyday people and everyday events of life more than in ivory towers or places of great power. She is at home with the powerless, which is one reason she is called a "friend of prophets." She hangs out with those who interfere with injustice buttressed by the status quo, and she sees the victims of injustice. She struggles for justice, therefore, and is herself, in Kingsley's words, citing an ancient poem of Parmenides, "the divine lawgiver of the universe."[7]

The universe is her home, her special domain; the cosmos is her mantle, which she wears creatively. This is clear from the poem above, in which wisdom's teachings are learned first from the design of the universe, and then from its elements, from time, from the sun, the seasons, the cycles of years, the stars, the animals, the beasts, the winds. Then – and *only then!* – from the "thoughts of humanity." Cosmology is the mother of wisdom. There is no wisdom without awareness of the cosmos. How wise this is, that humanity's thoughts are entirely predicated on all these other cosmic forces. Here, truly, is a naming of our common ancestry, the role of the cosmos in our lives. Human thoughts come very late to the cosmos and to wisdom. Plants and roots follow with their wisdom as well.

Can anyone be more cosmic than wisdom? Notice that wisdom is an artisan and a mother. The Divine Mother. No wonder there was no room for her in the patriarchal educational agendas of the past 300 years, when the feminine was banished or even worse, as in Francis Bacon's words, raped. "We shall torture mother earth for her secrets," he declared. At least he was honest about what the agenda without the feminine would entail.

Today is another (postmodern) day. We need to move beyond the neglect of and onslaught on Mother Wisdom that so characterized the modern world. How do we bring wisdom back to education?

CREATIVITY: THE KEY TO TEACHING WISDOM

A key is the role of creativity. Wisdom is not only artisan, but the maker of the world. She plays before the creation of the world. She is Eros at play. Only play draws in the imagination and creativity. She is play-full. You can tell how much a culture honours and seeks after wisdom by examining what role creativity, art, and imagination play in the educational project.

Art is key to the pedagogical revolution called for today. Not capitalist art – art as object or *objets d'art* or art as investment. No, not that kind of art – art as commodity and art as a consumer object. Art as soul work: *that's* what we need. Art as process, art as the making of connections and the drawing forth of the wisdom inside oneself, the wisdom inside all of us. "There is wisdom in all creative works," said the 12th-century musician, artist, scientist, and mystic Hildegard of Bingen. It is in creativity that wisdom will shine forth.

Creativity must be central to any postmodern educational form just as creativity was central to all pre-modern education. I do not know of a single aboriginal tribe on any continent – Australian, African, Celtic, North or South American, Asian, Pacific Island – where art and creativity were not at the heart of the teaching of their young. Ceremony and rituals were one such art form. So were dressing up of the body ("to match the beauty of the snake and the birds" as an Australian Aboriginal once told me), chanting of songs, drumming of drums, dancing on the earth. Learning and teaching were all about creativity. Not creativity in a vacuum and not creativity for the artists' sake, for ego sake, for fame sake, for salesmanship sake. No, none of that! It was creativity for the community's sake, creativity as a gift back to the Source, creativity as a Thank You. That is what drove human education for centuries and centuries.

Alas! We have wandered a long way from this truth. Today we hardly educate the imagination at all. When there is a budget crunch, out go the theatre courses and music courses and art department. They are expendable in the modern world consciousness. Aesthetics does not count for much. The media do all the imagining for us. They fill us with desires for products that our imaginations are taught to yearn for. They fill our empty souls for us. But that will not do. It is not working for more and more young people.

We have already remarked that children of colour are the least successful in our current educational models. This is not because "education is not a priority in their cultures." These ancient cultures all taught their kids just fine. Their cultures lasted thousands of years after all. The struggle is one of form. In an educational system that lacks creativity and cosmology as the twin pillars of learning, the soul is starved; the mind is bored; the spirit is squelched. Bring back creativity and cosmology – and with it wisdom – and far from being educational dropouts, these cultures will birth the new generation of leaders. I guarantee it.

FURTHER DIMENSIONS TO WISDOM

We have seen that wisdom is about justice, the cosmos, the feminine, and creativity and creation itself. Wisdom is more interested in *relationships* than in *things*. She is about inter-connectivity and connection-making. She rides the waves of relationships between beings and between time and space.

She is also about joy. The Book of Wisdom says, "Once you have grasped her, never let her go. In the end, she will transform herself into pure joy" (Sirach 6:27f.). She is also about passion for living, or biophilia, for it is said, "This is wisdom: to love life," and "whoever loves her loves life" (Sirach 4:12). Indeed, to find her is to find life (Proverbs 8:35). With wisdom, we are lovers of life; without wisdom, we are lovers of death in all its enticing dimensions. Without wisdom, we are set up for necrophilia or love of death, which is also our addictions. Every addiction is an attachment to something that kills us.

Wisdom is the "mother of all good things" (Wisdom 7:11) and she is about pleasure – she honours sexuality as theophany or experience of the Divine as in the Song of Songs found in the Hebrew Scriptures. She is not afraid of the lower chakras, neither the first chakra that links us to the earth through our feet and legs in dance, and to the cosmos with vibration; nor the second chakra, which is our sexuality; nor the third charka, which contains our righteous anger and moral indignation. She is at home in darkness – indeed, she honours the night in a special way, and the hidden, underground, in-depth secrets of our psyches.

She is close at hand – indeed, you will find her in your fourth chakra: She sits in the throne of your heart calling forth the good in you. She is herself beautiful and beauty: "Sophia I loved, I sought her out in my youth, I fell in love with her beauty, and I longed to make her my bride" (Wisdom 8:2). She is what we fall in love with, that experience of awe that entices us into our vocation and into our deepest relationships. Her home is the beauty of the universe itself and all its multiple manifestations. And she "plays everywhere in the world" (Proverbs 8:31) and takes delight in being with human beings.

In the East she is the mother of the Buddhas and in the West she is Mary the mother of God in Jesus. In the Christian tradition, she is the first name given to Jesus and the wisdom tradition is the ancestral tree from which the historical Jesus came. Ibn Al-Arabi, a 13th-century Muslim mystic, declared that "it is in the Image of the Creative Feminine that contemplation can apprehend the highest manifestation of God, namely creative divinity." In a Muslim practice called "recollection of Sophia," one learns anew how the feminine encompasses and combines the masculine.

WISDOM IN THE UNIVERSITY

In medieval Europe, when the university was invented, wisdom was named Queen of the Sciences and Queen of the University. All science was to direct itself to wisdom. Wisdom would judge it. When the great saint and scholar Thomas Aquinas received his chair in theology at the very first university, the University of Paris, he did so at a very young age. According to the practice of the time, it was his duty to deliver a formal inaugural lecture. He chose as his topic wisdom.

Wisdom, Aquinas teaches, "is manifest in creatures" and rules the cosmos. Wisdom has four tasks to perform, including revealing the mysteries of the Source of all things; producing creation "like an artist births art"; restoring creation; and perfecting creation. Wisdom is "of the heart" and is given us "on loan" – no one person and no one culture owns or possesses it. Wisdom comes from the prophets and accompanies justice, and while hidden and mysterious, nevertheless we all participate in it.[8]

Years ago I was asked to give a series of four lectures at the University of Vancouver and while I was free to choose the subjects of three of the lectures my opening topic was assigned: "Wisdom and the University." I sweated over that talk until the last minute, when I decided to tell the truth. My opening line was this: "Talking about wisdom in the university today is like talking about chastity in a brothel." With that I analyzed just why the modern university has banished wisdom – the banishment of the cosmos due to mechanistic science, the banishment of the feminine, the banishment of the heart and of creativity and more. We had a lively discussion that afternoon, but I wonder if our universities today are any more at home with wisdom than they were 20 years ago when I challenged that one school.

A Native American elder has said, "Only a madman thinks with his head." I might add, only a mad civilization thinks with its head...or educates people to think only with their heads. A healthy individual and a healthy educational system learn to think with heart as well as with head. Such a civilization thinks wisely.

A return to the love and living out of wisdom – wisdom as a way of life – this would mean a revival of philosophy and culture indeed. It would also shake up education linking the postmodern world to the pre-modern world like never before, and offering hope and possibility to a cynical and pessimistic species strangling on its knowledge and drowning in its own intellectual gravity.

5.

E: EDUCATION –
10 CS TO BALANCE THE 3 RS

Certain educators and politicians like to talk about "returning to the basics" in education, meaning the 3 Rs of "Reading, 'Riting, and 'Rithmetic." I believe we have to update our naming of the basics to balance the Reading, Writing, and Arithmetic, with what I call the 10 Cs of Education. These 10 Cs will ensure that we educate the whole human being and not just a small corner of one's brain (a corner of the left hemisphere).

We have called in this manifesto for an awe-based education, which is an ancestor-based and a wisdom-based education (the A and the W). In this section, we are considering methodology and pedagogy (the E of A.W.E). How to bring this about? The 10 Cs will bring it about. They constitute the revolution in education that we yearn for. They bring pre-modern wisdom together with postmodern needs, for our ancestors from pre-modern times invariably included these elements in the education of their young people.

The 10 Cs are the following: cosmology or creation (including ecology); contemplation; creativity or co-creation; chaos; compassion; courage or magnanimity; critical consciousness and judgment; community; ceremony and celebration; character and chakra development.

We shall consider each of these below.

1. Cosmology and ecology

Without knowing where we come from or when (that is, how long it took), we are lost. Cosmology teaches us where we come from, where "here" is, and therefore gives us a hint as to where we are headed. If we don't know our origins it is very difficult to be clear on our goals. Cosmology is about time and space.

We are gifted with a new cosmology today that, being offered by science, transcends nations, cultures, religions, and personality types. It is time to make this story come alive in the hearts and minds of our young people (and older ones, too). With cosmology, we reconnect with our inherent depths of immensity, intensity, and intimacy. To know the immensity of the universe (for example, that our galaxy is only one trillionth of the whole universe) is to be awakened to our vastness – but also to our specialness in the world.

Buckminster Fuller has observed that "becoming deliberately expansive instead of contractive, we ask, '*How* do we think in terms of *wholes?*' If it is true that the bigger the thinking becomes the more lastingly effective it is, we must ask, 'How big can we think?'" Fuller decried the modern thinking that begins with parts and "never reaches the whole." Rather, "in order to really understand what is going on, we have to abandon starting with parts, and we must work instead from the whole to the particulars." For "to learn anything you must start with the whole – with Universe. Comprehension of the whole alone leads to discovery of the significant intercomplementary functions to be played by the parts."[1]

Cosmology starts with the whole. To start with the whole is to appeal to what is natural in children because, as Fuller put it, children "want to understand the whole...Universe."[2] In this respect, Maria Montessori was a pioneer who did education right by emphasizing that "the important thing is to give a cosmic idea, one complete whole, the universe, for the child's mind...seeks not only facts but their underlying causes, and you cannot properly see the connections until you have first seen the whole."[3]

Cosmology creates a context. Context is so important. The modern age was more bent on text than on context.

The result is that we are, with the powers of knowledge and technology unleashed by modern education, destroying our very nest, which is the earth. By beginning with the whole, which is cosmology and with it ecology, a postmodern education sets the context for all we do and are, a perspective that has been sorely missing in modern consciousness, whether of politics, economics, religion, education, or morality. Anthropocentrism is not a context; it is an illusory way of seeing the world and of gerrymandering context to fit our projections and distortions and self-centred agendas.

What else happens when context is restored? Psychotherapist Estelle Frankel, who has been in practice listening to people's stories for 30 years, observes the following:

> I have learned that when we go beyond our personal predicaments and locate ourselves within the larger story, we open doors to the sacred dimension, and our lives become pregnant with meaning, living embodiments of Torah. We come to experience our lives as resonant with a much greater matrix of meaning, in which any transition we undergo, whether it be a death, divorce, illness, or disability, may initiate us into the larger mystery of life. [We also become] less alone in our suffering. We no longer see our personal struggles as simply personal; instead, we see them as mirroring a sacred process that occurs in all levels of creation, at all times.[4]

To hear how the universe unfolded in its 14 billion year history and how we have inherited that rich ancestry, and to begin to imagine how it is currently unfolding, and to ask what our role is as human beings in this continuous unfolding; to be baptized into the gratuitous beauty of this universe as a whole and this earth as a specific place and in a specific time in history – all of that is cosmology. And all of that will indeed bring meaning back to our lives, our struggles, and sacrifices. To reset our work and professions from politics to economics, from manufacturing to recreation, back into a cosmic and eco-context – there lies the bedrock for renewing our species and its education of present and future generations.

Thomas Berry tells us about the inherent connection between cosmology and ecology when he states that "ecology is functional cosmology." Ecology is the *local* expression of the cosmos; it is the small hoop that mirrors the large hoop. A society that has lost cosmology has lost a sense of ecology and its relationship to the earth. And an educational system that has neglected ecology has lost its relationship to the cosmos. To study cosmology is to study ecology and vice versa.

In a recent book, *Last Child in the Woods: Saving Our Children from Nature-Deficit Disorder*, Richard Louv argues that schools may teach children about the facts of the Amazon forest but do little to encourage children to explore nature that is right where they live. The author spent ten years travelling around the country, in both urban and rural areas, interviewing children and parents about their experiences in nature. Scientific research finds that children who are given early and ongoing positive exposure to nature thrive in ways that those cut off from nature do not. Nature-play reduces stress, sharpens concentration, develops healthy bodies, promotes creative problem solving, and can help heal attention-deficit disorder. It also develops one's sense of marvelling and of awe.

2. CONTEMPLATION, MEDITATION (KENOSIS, EMPTYING)

Maria Montessori teaches children how to "make silence." We need to explore the silence we are capable of making. Humans are all capable of "making silence." Making silence, calming our busy monkey brains and our action-reaction reptilian brains, is necessary for the very survival of our species as we live more and more in busy, crowded, noisy urban settings, and as we are called to deal more wisely with technological inventions that, if not checked, can annihilate our species with their immense powers of violence and destruction.

Many methods from wisdom traditions the world over can be used to teach practices of calming the busy brain, of meditation and stress reduction. One of our faculty members teaches Tai Chi and mask making, and has done so in prisons. In one such session, he was teaching a group of men all of whom had murdered people. When they finished class, several people said to him, "This is the first time in my life I have experienced quiet."

Wouldn't it be marvellous to introduce murderers to their capacities for quiet *before* they kill others? Wouldn't this education prove to be a marvellous investment in murder-prevention? And prison prevention? Studies and films are available that show what happens in a prison when meditation practices like *Vipassana* meditation is introduced to the prison complex. Calm displaces hyperactivity and hypertension. Joy begins to spread.

Why not teach joy and calm before prison and to the culture at large? Every human has these capacities in them, but they have to be nourished and nurtured. They have to be educed. That is education's job. Rather than feeding young people pills for so-called "hyperactivity," we ought to be showing them ways of finding peace that are internal and not by way of drug-taking. A person can take these ways with them their whole life.

In inner-city schools in San Francisco, yoga is being taught youngsters under the rubric of sports and physical fitness. A fourth grader reports, "I feel really grumpy in the morning. Yoga makes me feel ungrumpy." With yoga, students are calmer and stress is reduced. Children find inner controls. One teacher observes, "Yoga is similar to other sports in that it takes determination and will. It's different in that you compete with yourself. When kids see themselves improving, their self-esteem improves." As kids learn the exercises, they themselves lead the other students. Says one student, "When you can't focus, you do yoga and you can focus."[5]

Charles Burack, in an article on "Returning Meditation to Education," reports that getting students to simply focus on their breath produces powerful results that allow them to contemplate deeply. Engaging in such exercises provides a

> nonideological, nonauthoritarian, and nonconsumerist means of self-empowerment because it puts individuals in touch with their own deep, vital self, which is the living source of strength, wisdom, and kindness. This self is not selfish; rather, it is highly sensitive and responsive to the real needs and worth of the surrounding universe.[6]

The word *kenosis* means to be emptied. We can let go of an infinite amount of things; we humans are capable of vast emptying. We can empty the mind of bad memories and of anxious thoughts. Contemplative practices such as meditation exercises assist in such efforts to become empty. The Sufi poet Hafiz writes about how warriors (as opposed to mere soldiers) "tame the beasts in their past so that the night's hoofs can no longer break the jewelled vision in the heart" and how we also (for we are all potential warriors) "open every closet in the future and evict all the mind's ghosts who have the bad habit of barfing everywhere."[7]

Thirteenth-century philosopher Thomas Aquinas said the nearest thing to contemplation is play. Thus contemplative practice can and ought to lead to play and creativity.

3. CREATIVITY

Along with contemplation and emptying comes play, fantasy, and creativity. Creativity is utterly natural to our species – indeed it is the very working definition of who we are that anthropologists take with them into the field when they look for bones of old bipeds – bones that are accompanied by artifacts.

We are the biped who specializes in making artifacts. We are powerfully creative beings, which not only explains the beauty and genius we give birth to in our music, theatre, paintings, architecture, and science, but also explains our capacity for destruction or evil. A useful education today must instruct us in our creativity so that we do not turn it over to others, and so that we use it for purposes that are life-giving and life-affirming (biophilia) rather than destructive or death-affirming (necrophilia).

Too often, art classes are narrowly confined to developing specialized skills or producing objects. A pedagogy of creativity will teach art as process, not art as specialization or art as product-production. It will teach it to *all* students, not just to art majors. Entering into the relationship between colour, canvas, light, and the painter; between clay and the sculptor; between body and the dancer; between sound and the singer; between images and the poet – all of this is an essential part of an awe-based educational curriculum, one that will culminate in wisdom.

Time and again over my 30 years of teaching and overseeing teachers, I have seen students' lives turn around and become totally transformed by these process-oriented classes in creative arts. Art transforms; art heals; art offers the language by which to transform, awaken, and heal others.

We ought to be teaching about humanity's capacity for evil so that we can consciously move beyond it. Evil has everything to do with our capacity for creativity, with what we choose to do with it, and with our not turning it over to others. Gas ovens and hydrogen bombs are born of human creativity after all.

A postmodern marker of creativity is the cyber revolution, which we might say expresses the unique language and discovery of our postmodern times. Education needs to introduce the new generation to the wonders and possibilities of the computer and its potential creative uses. But in doing so we have to invite the young – whose skills at computers, cyberspace, and cam recorders are far more advanced than most of their elders' – to look on these new inventions not just with secular eyes, but with passion for the moral issues of our time and with questions about how cyberspace can contribute to the awakening of our species.

One student I met in the heart of the Silicon Valley wrote me these thoughts about the work and potential of the cyber world.

The emerging digital infrastructure, joined by the web, is becoming the global brain, with over a billion people on the web today, if you count wireless devices. While media, by themselves, are morally neutral, they can be put to the service of infinite good. You can research like-minded people in every country. You can convey experience with any media, including digital film, and deliver it instantaneously to almost anyone… The Tibetans have been preserving their archives with Mac and PCs for years. The *Dead Sea Scrolls* were translated and studied with a Macintosh. The translators were able to reduce years of labour down to hours… Technologies are being developed to bring people into alpha and delta states in seconds… In so far as digital technology can bring people together, it can foster compassion. It now gives the voice to the disenfranchised… Everyone now has instantaneous access to the Dalai Lama, thanks to the web. We are no longer captive to programming.[8]

In a postmodern educational setting, art skills will be practised daily, including but not limited to painting, dance, ritual-making, clay, song, chant, poetry, rap, video, theatre, and more. The new and ancestral creation stories and cosmology will provide the healthy content for these art experiences. That way, students develop their artistic skills and also engage at a deep and creative level with the learning of wisdom stories, even as they share them with others. In these postmodern times, the young take rapidly to technological skills, but it is up to the elders to provide substantial content and this program will assure that happens. Students become teachers through such self-expression.

A veritable "department of postmodern media" can be made available to students and "Festival Days" can be named that entice students to celebrate and put their skills and insights on display.

There is no reason why the older students cannot eventually also teach ancestral and contemporary cosmology stories they have learned to the younger students in a school, along with skills such as video making or rap or chant, thus spreading the word and also developing teaching and interpersonal skills. Special training can be offered the older students to prepare them to teach the younger ones.

One way in which we have been applying cyberspace technology and creativity to the needs of our time is in forms of ceremony or worship. For the past nine years, our Techno Cosmic Masses, now called "Cosmic Masses," have been utilizing DJs and VJs and electronic music, along with live instruments, song, dance, and rap, in order to reinvent worship and make it live again. These inventions invite the young into leadership or priestly roles in worship, while they liven worship for people of all ages; they bring beauty alive once again.

Creativity is also about problem solving. When we look at the ecological crises that face our species today, we sometimes despair or throw up our arms and declare "This is too much; this is beyond me to solve." But by working together and by making ecology a priority, we can solve many problems. Carl Pope, the executive director of the Sierra Club, points out that if the federal government simply required automakers to use the best available technology, "all vehicles could average 40 miles per gallon within 10 years." And if one in ten Americans regularly used public transit, the United States would reduce its oil consumption by 40 percent. We can do this since one-third of California residents responded to the 2001 energy crisis by reducing their energy consumption by at least 20 percent.[9]

4. Chaos and Darkness

What science calls chaos and the mystical tradition calls the *via negativa*, or the "dark night of the soul," is with us everywhere today. But science assures us – and the mystics assure us – that darkness, unravelling, not being in control, confusion, doubt and uncertainty, in other words chaos, are natural rhythms in nature and part of a dialectic of expansion and contraction. Indeed, chaos or the *via negativa* offer us rich occasions for learning life's deepest lessons: lessons of trust and wonder and waiting and gestation. A useful education today should prepare us for such times.

Chaos is part of nature. It is part of weather systems, the unfolding of galaxies, supernova explosions, and black holes.[10] It is also part of human nature. A midwife told me recently that "Nothing is more chaotic than childbirth. It is a mess. But observe what comes from it." New beings come through chaos and our lives are marked by many chaotic episodes. Chaos is not a "bad" thing. But it is a mark of the universe that we must be prepared and educated for.

The arts of letting be and of letting go are part of the inheritance of the human species. Every culture has ways to teach letting be and letting go. These need to be included in the pedagogy of all our education, from childhood through professional schooling.

Chaos is part of human creativity in a special way. Artists recycle chaos. The creative process is often a passage through chaos. If all are artists, then all can expect chaos. We need to educate for it, especially at this time in history.

The poet Rilke names a genuine reality that many of us are feeling at this time in history when he says, "Life is heavier than the weight of all things." He is right. Sometimes life does indeed feel heavier than the weight of all things. When species disappear at unheard of rates, when global warming threatens cities and whole nations as we know them (it is likely that when the warming currents of the Pacific Ocean are altered by global warming, Ireland will become as cold as Siberia), when starvation faces a third of the world while another third are becoming obese from overeating, when hurricanes wipe out cities and tsunamis do the same in minutes, life does indeed seem dark and heavy. The mystics talk about such times as a "dark night of the soul."

Today our species is in a collective dark night of the soul. We are captive to so many forces over which we feel we have no control, that we are, like John of the Cross in the 16th century, imprisoned. Rabbi Heschel proposed that we not talk about just the "dark night of the soul" but about the "dark night of society." And I propose and believe that we are living through a time that can rightly be named the "dark night of our species." By acknowledging its reality, we can prepare ourselves to learn from it and even move beyond it.

The first lesson of the dark night is not to run. The Sufi poet Hafiz teaches us how the spiritual warrior refuses to run.

> Love wants to reach out and manhandle us, break all our teacup talk of God... The Beloved sometimes wants to do us a great favour: hold us upside down and shake all the nonsense out. But when we hear He

is in such a "playful drunken mood" most everyone
I know quickly packs their bags and hightails it out
of town.[11]

Darkness has a lot to teach us. We need to stick around in
order to learn. And we as a species have a lot to learn at this
time about the deeper lessons of living and of being human.
Among the lessons to learn are the following:

- ☞ The dark night as a learning place;
- ☞ The softening and watering of the heart;
- ☞ The awakening of imagination, play, and the quest
  for repose;
- ☞ The purification of our longing – What do we truly
  cherish, truly long for? What sacrifices are we willing to undergo for the Beloved, the object of our
  longing?

The purpose of the dark night of the soul and dark night of
our species may be to render us all shamans.

In this regard, we might learn from the Navajo artist
David Palladin, who as a young man joined the army and was
captured by the Nazis. He was put in a concentration camp for
four years, where he underwent supreme torture and agony.
When the allies liberated the camp, Palladin was comatose,
paraplegic and weighed 64 pounds. After coming out of the
coma two years later and being cured by the medicine of his
elders, he lived a full and productive life as a painter, writer,

and eventually as a minister. Toward the end of his life he told what his elders had taught him: that his extreme suffering in the concentration camp was a school or initiation to teach him to become a shaman. He said, "Shamans know that those wounds are not theirs but the world's. Those pains are not theirs but Mother Earth's. You can gift the world as shaman because you're a wounded warrior. A wounded healer and a wounded warrior are one." So instead of returning pain for pain and action with reaction, the warrior-shaman raises above his own dead body and says, "I have died, too. Now let's dance. We're free. The spirit is ours because we have died. Now we are resurrected from the ashes."[12]

We may be involved as a species today in a collective dark night – an agony and a torture – because we have this lesson to learn: that of becoming shamans and healers.

Of course, as humans, we bring some chaos upon ourselves. We create unnecessary chaos. Our creativity does this. Wars, for example, and any explosions of violence, are sure to result in breakdowns of relationships and to cause both external and internal chaotic conditions. Global warming and the hurricanes and dislocation of peoples it brings with it, the waves of migration that occur when soil dries up and agriculture is threatened, wars in oil-rich nations... all derive from an unnecessary dependence on fossil fuels.

Education in creativity must also be, therefore, education in our capacity – as a species and as individuals – for evil. Evil is what humans create when they prefer destruction over construction and the individual "I" over the common good or the good of others. We are all capable of evil. No individual and no tribe is exempt from it. We ought to study it; for evil, just as creativity, marks us as a species. Our species is capable of great evil. Why wouldn't we want to learn about it in order not to add chaos on top of chaos? And in order to interfere with evil and stand in the way of evil as effectively as we can.

Consider just one invention of the 20th century: the atomic bomb. Henry Wiseman comments on the deeper meaning of the atomic bomb dropping on Japan, in 1945, when he writes,

> The bomb that fell on Hiroshima cut history in two like a knife. Before and after are two different worlds. That cut is more abrupt, decisive, and revolutionary than the cut made by the star over Bethlehem… The economic and political order fitted to the age before the parachute fell becomes suicidal in the age coming after. The same breach extends into education and religion.[13]

Arthur Koestler observes that

> from the dawn of consciousness until 6 August 1945, man had to live with the prospect of his death as an

individual; since the day when the first atomic bomb outshone the sun over Hiroshima, he has had to live with the prospect of his extinction as a species.[14]

According to Robert J. Lifton, this stark reality has introduced on a massive scale a kind of "vast breakdown of faith in the larger human matrix supporting each individual life, and therefore a loss of faith (of trust) in the structure of human existence." With this loss of trust there comes a kind of appeal to necrophilia and a distancing from biophilia, what Lifton calls "the replacement of the natural order of living and dying with an unnatural order of death-dominated life." [15]

And yet, paradoxically, our dance with folly and with mass extinction can also lead to a waking up and a wisdom, as Lifton also testifies: "Hiroshima was the prelude to all this – an expression of technological evil and madness which could, but will not necessarily, be a path to wisdom." [16] Yes, madness can be a path to wisdom. Are we up to it? For it can also be simply... a path to more madness.

5. COMPASSION

There is universal agreement from all the world's wisdom traditions that the best humankind has to offer is compassion and that compassion is not beyond our capabilities.

The Dalai Lama summarizes this teaching when he declares that "We can reject everything else: religion, ideology, all received wisdom. But we cannot escape the necessity of love and compassion." From Buddha to Jesus, from Isaiah to Muhammad, from Black Elk to the Vedas of India, from Lao Tzu to the wisdom teachers of Africa, our species is admonished to respond to life with compassion. Gandhi and Martin Luther King, Jr. are just two who have become 20th-century heroes for having done so.

Compassion is the living out of our interdependence (in today's physics and cosmology, interdependence is once again the basis of all our relations). Compassion is about sharing the joy and sharing the pain, and about doing what we can to relieve the pain, especially that caused by injustices, whether they be ecological, economic, social, racial, gender, or generational in nature. Compassion requires the calling forth, the educing, the educating, therefore, of our deepest capacities as a species – our capacity to act as if we truly are part and parcel of one another, in joy as well as in sorrow.

Compassion calls us to create a society where all are winners and none are losers, a "world that works for everyone," as Sharif Abdullah puts it. This means creating an economic system, a political system, a healthcare system, an educational system, where we all have a fair chance and where the dispossessed are not forgotten.

Is that possible? Is that a pipe dream? It is impossible if we fail to educate as if it were possible. But how can it be impossible if all the religious traditions of the world espouse it as possible? It is possible if we set our goals that way and if we lay out our educational strategies in that direction. It is not possible if it is ignored or if we develop no strategies to bring it about. Or if education is busy serving hidden and uncriticized agendas of empire building, or gender, tribal, racial, religious, or economic hegemonies.

Compassion means justice. That is the ancient teaching, the pre-modern teaching about compassion. (In the modern era, compassion no longer meant a relationship between equals; it became divorced from justice.) Another very current word for justice – and therefore for compassion – is *sustainability*. Compassion is what is ultimately sustainable. Injustice is, in the long run, unsustainable.

An example of contemporary education in compassion can be found in the work of a doctoral student at University of Creation Spirituality, who holds a PhD in Applied Quantum Mechanics from the Electrical and Computer Engineering Department of the University of California at Santa Barbara. She is currently teaching teenagers to develop green or sustainable technologies. She has started an organization called Natura or Nature-Affirming-Technology. Natura gives students practical experience with current "green" technology methods and concepts, as well as local and global perspectives on environmental problems. Students participate in hands-on sustainable science and technology so that theory is connected to practice. The hope that practice brings overcomes the despair that the young often feel on hearing of the environmental crisis. Students build solar ovens and design and install solar electric systems, and learn their own powers of creativity in the process. Such programs deserve to be multiplied throughout the country.

6. Courage

Compassion is not possible if we lack courage. Courage, as Aquinas taught, is the most basic of all moral virtues; without courage, no other virtue is sustained or sustainable.

Fear will accomplish little or nothing and it will taint whatever it touches. Courage stands up to fear. None of the 10 Cs we are speaking about will be brought into education or into practice if we cannot stand up to fear, and work out of courage.

The word courage comes from the French for a "large heart." We need to expand our hearts. Cosmology helps us to do that; so, too, do letting go, facing chaos and darkness, increasing our sense of awe, and increasing our works of creativity and compassion – all of which expands the heart. Courage is what the "spiritual warrior" or "prophet" majors in.

Some people ask: How do you teach courage? Is courage teachable? First, we can study the lives of courageous people and the teachings of the wisdom traditions. The latter, in particular, can teach us how to develop the prophetic and warrior side of ourselves, and how to encourage its development in ourselves and in others. In these ways we can teach courage. Creativity also expands the heart and what M. C. Richards calls "moral imagination," and that, too, develops courage.

We can also interview and ask questions of persons of courage. For example, I met Rev. Fred Shuttlesworth this past year. Shuttlesworth was a Civil Rights minister in Birmingham, Alabama, during the most dire times of Ku Klux Klan resistance to civil rights. The Klan bombed his house; they beat him with chains three times; and sheriff Bull O'Connor arrested his eight- and ten-year-old children. I asked Rev. Shuttlesworth, "Where did you get your courage?" He replied, "You can call it courage. But it really was trust. When they bombed my house and I walked out of it alive I said to myself, 'They cannot kill me.' Oh, they might kill my body, but they cannot kill me." He knew, from then on, that the Civil Rights Movement could not be stopped.

Courage, like any virtue, takes practice. Part of education is allowing one another to practise our values and to stand up for them – to find a voice. Being supported as one finds one's voice develops courage. So, too, do practices of letting go and letting be. Tasting calmness and learning to be at home with solitude – all these practices represent ways to grow in courage.

Courage is also found in community. Being with others who share your values is a great support when it comes time to take courageous action. The courageous person need not be a loner (at least not most of the time) provided one has found a courageous community to share with. And that increases the joy and the fun of it all.

7. CRITICAL CONSCIOUSNESS AND JUDGMENT

To use the brains we have all been given means that we learn to think critically. The word *critical* comes from the Greek word *kritein*, to judge. We all must be able to make judgments and to think critically, to think beyond the myths and illusions that our culture might feed us. We have to weigh in our own minds what is applicable to our life and times, as Ernest Becker puts it.

Does education prepare us for this critical thinking? Becker thinks not.

No State has trained its youth to be the responsible critics of their own society, and so we have revolution and war and repression and more war. Revolution, war, repression: these are synonyms of the failure to educate youth in the capacity peacefully and freely to remake the world... No particular ideology is involved: Neither capitalism nor communism nor socialism nor Nazism. The State is to blame...[17]

In blaming "the state," Becker is in fact blaming education that the state sponsors. He is saying that education is too often uncritical; it does not train students to think and that means, among other things, to judge. Judging is, after all, what ethics is about – making judgments and making decisions. Humans need practice at this. Answers cannot come from the outside in, but must come from the inside out. That is what having a conscience means: to judge; to decide; to weigh; to be critical.

In our time, we don't just need compassion; we need critical compassion. Not sentimental or squishy compassion, but *critical* compassion. Compassion that passes through our best capacities for weighing and judgment and critical mindedness. When we fail to do this, Becker believes, the inevitable happens and

> as a result, the industrial masses in Fascist countries are swayed by demagogues; the industrial masses in Communist countries are swayed by commissars; the industrial masses in capitalist countries are swayed by the uncritical commercial ideology that controls the mass media. And democracy, after all, is the true government by oratory as Hobbes warned, where the few sway the uncritical passions of the many. The historical problem is no longer a problem of the "right ideology" for modern man: the problem is to convert the socially liberated masses in every modern State

into educationally "liberated" ones. The problem is to give them the freedom in ideas and criticism that turn them against those who tyrannically control the State, whether it be the commercial mass media, the demagogues, or the commissars. In this sense, no people on earth is today free, no matter what its ideology.[18]

These observations become all the more significant since they were uttered 45 years ago, before the fall of the Berlin Wall and much of communist ideology. They are crucial because they address – more than ever – the pitfalls of the "commercial mass media," which have become far more influential rather than less since Becker's words were written and since communism collapsed. The mass media have more and more taken over the world and they face very little resistance except for the Internet.

David Korten has collected data from polls indicating that, right wing ideology to the contrary, a consensus exists in America about many of the most pressing social issues. He has found that 83 percent of Americans fear the decline in family life and believe that we need to rebuild neighbourhoods and small communities; 93 percent agree we are too focused on working and making money and not focused enough on family and community; 86 percent feel we are too focused on getting what we want now and are ignoring the needs of future generations; 78 percent feel advertising and marketing is putting too much pressure on children to buy things that are unhealthy or unnecessary; 90 percent of children say friends and family are "way more important" than the things money can buy; only 13 percent wished their parents made more money; 87 percent believe we need to treat the planet as a living system and that we should have more respect and reverence for nature; and 68 percent would be willing to return to a simpler way of life in order to improve the health of the environment.[19]

The work of Elaine Risler and other scholars of pre-patriarchal times indicates that we do not have to take it for granted, as we have for 6500 years, that men need to rule the world. There were times in the past when women oversaw cultures (the Iroquois nation was such an arrangement) and when *domination* took second place to *partnership*. We can choose partnership over domination – as many are trying to do in our time.

To be true to the principle of critical awareness or critical compassion is to face evil head-on. Becker proposes a curriculum that awakens our capacity for criticism and therefore for engaged and participatory citizenship. Says Becker: "A curriculum centered on the idea of alienation...gives us continuing self-criticism, and leaves our future wholly open... We need to develop in the student a fully critical 'sense of State.'"[20] In a rarely optimistic moment, Becker exclaims that focusing on alienation will produce nothing less than "mass-elitism! What is more excellent than teaching everyone the causes of their lack of freedom? What is more democratic than freeing the energies of all men?... What is excellent knowledge, except knowledge that has a truly critical quality?"[21] Such a focus provides a "truly aristocratic model of the masses: It gives us continuing self-criticism, and leaves our future wholly open."[22] Healthy criticism liberates.

8. COMMUNITY

Everything we have spoken of in the search for an awe-based and wisdom-based education that incorporates the "10 Cs of Education" has to do with rediscovering and reliving community. Community is natural to ourselves and to the rest of nature. The word comes from two Latin words that mean "to share a common task." In community, co-workers share a struggle to see compassion happen, including the shared celebration of life. Justice and creativity are integral to community. And cosmology names the most basic community of all.

The modern era explored areas of individual rights and the dignity of the individual and that is knowledge well-attained. But for a postmodern time we must balance the individual with community once again, for humans are happiest in community where they share the most, whether it be the joys of life or the tragedies of life. Celebration and grief both find their outlet in community. And our ultimate moral responsibility is to pass on a world of beauty and health to communities that are not yet born but are promised to be born. Our ancestors seven generations from now are the ones – they are the community – to judge the morality of our actions today. We should have them in mind just as we hold our ancestors in mind. For we are the ancestors of subsequent communities.

We have much to learn from the pre-modern world, which more or less succeeded in teaching about community – not only humans in community with other humans, but humans in community with other earth creatures. Becker sees history as "the problem of the decline of community." He recognizes that the loss of community began

> when the integral primitive communities began their inevitable breakup. It was then that daily life became more and more separated from the cover of divine meanings, from an integral pattern of myth and ritual that consecrated most of the important acts of the individual in community. With this breakup, man lost his firm rooting in the divine ground, his daily life became increasingly secular – which means increasingly narrow and hollow, increasingly pragmatic, increasingly autonomous. It was here that the cumulative "terror of history" began to make itself felt. Man had lost his contact with continual natural

cosmic rhythms; he ceased to be nourished in the feeling that his life was transcendentally significant; the anxious burden of "sin" thus pervades more and more of his daily cares.[23]

One wonders if this loss of community – thoroughly exacerbated by Newtonian physics which pits atom against atom in rugged individualistic competition – does not help to explain the success of fundamentalism in our time. Globally and in all religious faiths, fundamentalism is on the rise and often in scary ways. One thing fundamentalism offers is a kind of instant and total community (albeit of a pseudo kind, one that is built on hatred of other groups, scapegoating, and fear). Fundamentalism is always "us against them," which makes for an intense bonding among the "us." Fundamentalism is also driven by an intense salvation compulsion – so and so saves me from ever-present sin. The "Rapture" is an archetypal utterance of this idea that only a few will be saved – and that few is, of course, us, and not them.

Religion often embraces fundamentalism by preaching cheap guilt and thus instructing the masses in a lethal combination of cosmic loneliness, separateness, and guilt. Critical believers are then driven away as heretics or the "other" (the "them"), and religion carries on its crusades enlisting others who may or may not be of their faith persuasion. It is telling, I believe, that just as Jerry Falwell and Pat Robertson's first response to the 9/11 disaster was to say that God was getting even with America because of feminists and homosexuals, so too, Muslim fundamentalist preachers have been telling their flocks in Indonesia that the tsunami occurred because of their sins.

What the fundamentalists have in common – fear and scapegoating, guilt and negative messages about women – overpowers their differences. Control of chaos seems to be their bottom line, whether they be of the Taliban, Vatican, or Pat Robertson variety. Those of more mature faith then move increasingly into spirituality and let religion go, when religion embarrasses itself and all it claims to represent, when it constructs ideologies of sin and salvation in preference to stories of blessing, goodness, empowerment, creativity, justice, and joy. Compassion goes out the stained glass window. (Thomas Aquinas says that fear is so powerful an emotion that it renders compassion impossible.) In the process, religion ignores its true duties, which are to create ritual and community among all peoples and all beings – "all our relations," that is, all of creation – and to teach the way to community, which is justice and compassion.

Becker believes that from the ashes of individualism sown in the modern era there can emerge a true sense of community in the postmodern era.

The terror of history yielded one great fruit: the development of individualism, out of the decline of

> community...we must find a way to reunite history and individualism with the transcendent meaning in community...we need to combine Socratic self-reliance with a new life-giving myth in a new community.[24]

This life-giving myth surely is the newly found truth of the interdependence of all beings, which is a very ancient truth as we have seen.

From this newly found sense of community there will derive a greater sense of meaning in life and of shared ethics, as Becker predicts.

> The life of freemen in community must be united by a myth of the meaning of life itself, a truly dynamic and creative myth. This would unite our whole perspective by giving our education its ultimate and agreed ethical grounding in the most forceful and creative way possible.[25]

Speaking of community, it would do us well to understand the global context that forms the matrix for our species today. If you imagine the human population of the Earth as a village of 100 people, it would look something like the following:

☞ There would be 57 Asians, 21 Europeans, 14 Americans (North and South), 8 Africans.

- There would be 52 women and 48 men.
- There would be 70 people of colour and 30 Caucasians.
- There would be 89 heterosexuals and 11 homosexuals.
- There would be six people owning 59 percent of the entire world's wealth and all of them would be from the United States of America.
- There would be 80 living in bad living conditions.
- There would be 70 undereducated.
- There would be 50 underfed.
- One would die.
- Two would be born.
- Only one would have higher education.
- Only one would have a computer.
- If you have never suffered a war, a jail cell, torture, or hunger, you are better off than 500 million people the world over.
- If you can enter a church, synagogue, or mosque without fear of jail or death, you are better off than three million people in the world.
- If there is food in your refrigerator, if you have shoes and clothes, a bed and a roof, you are richer than 75 percent of the people in the world.
- If you have a bank account and money in your wallet, you belong to the eight percent of the people in the world who are well-to-do.

9. Ceremony, celebration, and ritual

There is no community without ceremony and ritual. This observation by African teacher Malidoma Some is so real and so important. If we want community we must teach ceremony and ritual.

Community includes the sharing of all in the tribe – the sharing of the joys and of the sorrows. It includes the building up of strength and courage to carry on. All this takes place in ceremony and ritual. One African American woman was interviewed recently about her days in the Civil Rights Movement 40 years ago. She said, "Martin Luther King took the fear away from us." That is what made the celebrations and ceremonies in church with Dr. King so effective; they displaced fear with courage and set the marchers on their way. It also shows the powerful effect of authentic elders (even though King did not live to reach the age of 40). Are the elders of today leading in courage?

Ancient peoples taught their children primarily through ceremonies. Ceremonies were intergenerational; the elders assisted the young. This working together of elders and youth is needed today on a grand scale. But one of the most serious problems we face is that we have had a loss of eldership, thanks to the breakdown of community and the destruction of indigenous communities. The older ones today, not having themselves undergone rites of passage and other transformative ceremonies, are in a bad place to be leading the young.

Furthermore, in Western cultures especially, the elders are often choosing to "retire" away from and separated from the young, effectively leaving the young to fend for themselves.

I believe the word *retirement* is one of the most obscene words in our lexicon. We ought to replace it with "refirement." When adults reach an age when they no longer have to fight daily to make a living for themselves and their family, they ought not to retire but rather get themselves "refired up" – find new life, new visions, new invitations to serve the younger generation. That is what wisdom is always about after all; it is something passed on from generation to generation. Many are the young people today who yearn for elderly companionship, direction, and guidance. But elders are too often impossible to find. Many are lost on the golf courses, or in the financial money-making marketplace, rather than being in touch with the new generation. Yet the new generation needs their wisdom and presence among them. It is mutual. The fire of the young can re-fire the adults. The refirement of the adults can fire up the young and give direction to their passion.

We need ceremonies at all times of our lives: At birth and at death, at puberty and at marriage, at divorce and at retirement/refirement, at graduations and at healings, it is part of being human to seek out and receive gifts of ceremonies. Authentic ceremonies recharge us, heal us, energize us, amaze us. They release our best capacities for compassion and service, for learning and teaching. They demarcate and honour beginnings and endings. They re-member and re-connect with the ancestors, ushering them among us.

It is through ceremony that the biggest stories, such as those of the universe itself or of our great ancestors, are most effectively carried on. Are we ready to bring ceremony back to education? We must be. Ceremony is part and parcel of the postmodern awareness, not least of all because it is so integral to pre-modern consciousness.

10. Character and chakra development

These 10 Cs of education prepare the groundwork for character development and moral development. They are not sectarian or religious as such. They are humanitarian and represent universal values that can assure our sustainability as a species on this endangered planet. Buckminster Fuller is an example of this. It is said that he valued

> *the power of personal integrity* as a force in the world, available to each of us, that transcends our "position" in life, our particular abilities and skills, and the specific circumstances in which we find ourselves. He saw this power of personal integrity as a force capable of steering humanity towards the realization of a world that truly works for everybody.[26]

Indeed, Fuller described our current crisis as a species using educational jargon. He saw it as an "exam" when he said,

> The present evolutionary crisis of humans on planet Earth is that of a final examination for their continuance in Universe. It is not an examination of political, economic, or religious systems but of the integrity of each and all individual humans' responsible thinking and unselfish, response to the acceleration in evolution's ever more unprecedented events.[27]

Thus it is our integrity that will see us through that test.

To be cosmically aware and ecologically grateful and reverent; to be at home with calm and contemplation; to be creative and alive with imagination; not to run from chaos but to undergo chaos; to be compassionate; to be courageous and magnanimous; to be critically conscious and to possess a developed conscience; to be community-aware and willing to serve the community; to develop and undergo ceremony and ritual – all this is about character development. It is about developing inner disciplines and about putting one's values into practice. Our educational institutions need to teach such character development.

It is not as if our culture is not teaching its own version of character and virtue. As David Korten analyzes the situation, it has been doing so for 5000 years.

Faced with the organizational challenge of dealing with growing population densities, our forebears made a choice for the dominator relations of Empire. A self-destructive era of warfare, greed, racism, sexism, and suppression of the higher orders of human consciousness followed.[28]

As James Garrison puts it, "Our educational institutions prepare us for social responsibility by giving us facts, refusing to teach values other than the virtues of competition and dominance." It is not wisdom, alas, that is being taught, but its opposite.

The modern world emphasizes the manipulative, rational, and formulating capacities of consciousness – essentially the masculine in its negative aspects. We have been taught to relate to the world through the head, seeking control, rather than by balancing the head with the heart in the pursuit of harmony within a greater whole.[29]

Harmony within a greater whole – that is wisdom. Do we want to pursue and teach our children to pursue the values of the empire? Or do we want to pursue the values of earth community?

One fresh way to conceive of character development is to borrow language from the East, which has identified the chakras of our bodies and psyches as important centre points of healthy power. True education is educing authentic power and ability from each student. Are we educating all the chakras in our educational systems today? I think not.

The modern age put all education into just the head chakra, in fact in the left hemisphere of the brain, which is the sixth chakra narrowly conceived. Rationality abounds. Tests and exams are multiplied. The pre-modern age did not restrict education so much to the head alone. Monastic education, for example, incorporated working the fields and chanting along with intellectual studies. Native American children learned in the woods, along with the animals and birds, trees and fauna. Sitting in desks is not the sole way to learn. Ancestral Wisdom Education (A.W.E.) will make room for educating all seven chakras.

That education will pay attention to the following:

- 1st chakra: educating for cosmology and healthy pride (and against couchpotatoitis [*acedia*] and arrogance), relating to earth and to all vibrations of the universe (cosmology)

- 2nd chakra: educating for balance and the generativity that results (and against power trips that employ lust as a weapon, or that preach a repression and fear of lust)

- ☞ 3rd chakra: educating for strength, grounding, and positive use of anger and moral outrage (and against violence)
- ☞ 4th chakra: educating for compassion and forgiveness and overcoming of fear
- ☞ 5th chakra: educating for speaking out and telling one's wisdom (instead of gluttony and its postmodern equivalent, consumerism that stuffs one's wisdom down one's throat)
- ☞ 6th chakra: educating for intuition and for intellectual analysis (and against one-sided rationalism masquerading as intellectual life and education)
- ☞ 7th chakra: educating for community with all beings (and against envy)[30]

To educate all the chakras once again: that must be a working goal of any postmodern education, of any effort at awe-based and wisdom-based education.

Character building is about developing moral citizens. Morality is not something subjective as it was thought to be in the modern era. Morality is about community, its survival and sustainability. It is about service and justice and compassion, and not about passivity and taking for granted or hoarding. Morality is the habits and practices we require to survive as a species.

Becker comments as follows:

The logical positivists may be content to live in a scientific world, and only a scientific world – but most people also want to live in a moral world; and we know only too bitterly that so far science has hardly helped this broader ambition… What we need and have wanted…is nothing less than a solution to the problem of community, of social morality, of ordered society. This is the great abyss at the heart of modern life that opened up with the decline of the mediaeval cosmology and of the medieval community that it tried unsuccessfully to hold together.[31]

Yes, education is looking into a "great abyss." And we dare not turn away. Education bears an immense responsibility, an immense moral responsibility. Becker talks about the university becoming a "seat of a New Moral View of the World."

Only in this way can the university be revitalized, by becoming the seat of a New Moral View of the World. Nothing less. This is the heart of man, the heart of education, the heart of the social problem, Morality. This is also what has been smoldering underneath all discussions of what the university should be and do; although only a few have dared to say it. John Henry Newman did, and frankly called for

knowledge of the true relations of things, knowledge
as philosophy, knowledge for right choice.[32]

Korten names that right choice as a choice in favour of earth
community, with all that entails, including true democracy
and an economic system that works for everyone, not just a
chosen few.

Morality is also an aesthetic issue for both Becker and
for philosopher bell hooks. Becker writes: "human morality
is a problem in aesthetics, a problem of man's striving for
maximum meaning… We can say, then, that man's ideal
moral problems are also his ideal aesthetic problems."[33] bell
hooks declares that the link between the "black underclass"
and the intellectual is aesthetics, and that the "next revolution" will be a revolution in aesthetics.

Aesthetics is not what Madison Avenue or Hollywood
tells us aesthetics is. Aesthetics is more participatory than
that. An aesthetic dimension to morality must be balanced
by a critical consciousness toward society. That is a justice
test. What is uglier than injustice? What is uglier than the
destruction of beauty, be that beauty the glory of an ancient
forest, the grace of an eagle, or the mind of a youngster. What
is uglier than the destruction of the lung capacity of a baby
by polluted air, or the killing of youngsters by youngsters
because despair has taken over their souls or their neighbourhoods? Injustice is just plain ugly.

And justice is beautiful – it is, like beauty, harmonious, joyful, and shareable. Something to praise. It arouses celebration. Justice, like beauty, is also sustainable. Justice preserves beauty in all its forms.

Conclusion
YELLAWE –
Youth and Elders Learning Laboratory for Ancestral Wisdom Education

A manifesto, as I said earlier, is a "making manifest" of what is in fact quite obvious. A manifesto tries to tell the truth.

In this manifesto I have tried to say what is actually quite evident: that education, as important as it is for our species, is not working. That is, the forms and pedagogy we are employing are not working. Education is not working for the young or for adults; it is not working for the planet, with its endangered species and forests and topsoil; or for inner-city children who are more likely to end up in prison (because education failed them) than in college.

We can do better – much better.

We can deliver meaningful instead of meaningless education; we can provide mindful instead of mindless education. I have listed ways to do so, ways that have been tested for many years where I have taught and overseen programs for adults in America. These ways are in many respects ancient and tested by our pre-modern ancestors.

We might summarize the passage that we are undergoing as a species in the following manner:

- from modern to postmodern (including pre-modern)
- from empire to community
- from knowledge to wisdom
- from law to justice
- from commerce to stewardship
- from religion to spirituality
- from education to learning
- from making money to making awe
- from greed to gratitude
- from anthropocentric to cosmic and ecological

The problem – and the solution for education – is more about *form* than it is about individuals; it is about pedagogy. The solutions, therefore, are not to be found in blaming educators nor in demanding more and more "testing" of students. *The solutions are to be found in seeking wisdom instead of just knowl-*

edge; in creating awe-based learning since awe is what awak-
ens the mind and heart just as good smells awaken the appetite.
Real education builds on the inherent curiosity in all humans to
know and explore our ancestors – the human and the more-than-
human ancestors – and to do so in the context of our own survival
needs.

We have laid out here a ten-point plan, the "10 Cs of Education," which speak to the revolution in pedagogy that is needed at this time in history. The two pillars of the 10 Cs are cosmology and creativity. For this is how both awe and empowerment flow again. The revolution of which I speak is not just for children but must catch the minds and souls of adult learners and teachers, politicians and tax-paying citizens as well, for they are all educators to the upcoming generation. We must train the heart along with the head. We must have a wisdom-based education. That alone will save our species, save the planet from our species, and preserve the planet in its health and beauty for generations that follow.

Time is running out.

I am not the only one speaking about or applying this kind of pedagogy. I give great credit to the Waldorf educational tradition for employing many of these elements in their successful educational techniques. I give credit to Maria Montessori for her profound efforts similarly. I have hope that not only public schools but also the growing number of charter schools will sit up and take notice of the 10 Cs of Education; I have hope that they will commit to critiquing the forms and pedagogy of educational systems we can no longer presume are doing a healthy thing for the young, or for the culture that needs to be born.

YELLAWE

I am committing myself to working with young people who recognize the power of this revolution, who want to educate the next generation, and who carry the skills of postmodern language that can have an impact as "edutainment." Indeed, one of these people, "Professor Pitt," a 31-year-old African American rapper, video maker, and martial arts practitioner, has put the themes of this book, including the 10 Cs, to rap and video. Working together, we will begin an alternative educational model not by challenging public schools head-on, but by offering courses after school hours. That way, educators need not feel personally threatened. We will offer an alternative model that some day will penetrate even our educational bureaucracies. That way we follow the advice of Buckminster Fuller, who proposed that those who want to bring about social change should do so not by frontal attack, but by offering better models. Fuller said, "You never change things by fighting the existing reality. To change something, build a new model that makes the existing model obsolete."

We will call this project YELLAWE, which stands for

Youth and
Elders'
Learning
Laboratory of
Ancestral
Wisdom
Education

Let me break this down a bit. First, it is so important at this
time that young people and older people work together and
learn from each other, that they pool their wisdom and their
concerns. At this cusp between the modern and the postmodern worlds, the young hold the new *language* of imagery,
computers, cybertechnology, media, DJ, VJ, and more. But it
is the elders' task to have imbibed some of the most important
stories from the past and in so doing to provide some worth-
while *content*. It is the task of older ones to throw off the notion
of retirement and take on the mantle of "refirement"; to move
from the illusion that one's late years are meant to be spent on
golf courses and filling up in restaurants or playing the stock
market, and instead to give back to the younger generation. To
give one must be working-with. Elders and youth must work
together today like never before to call up ancient wisdom and
to create new wisdom for our common survival.

Calling this effort a *learning laboratory* instead of a *school*
or *university* or *educational project* is deliberate. Learning –
alas! – is different from education. Education, like church,

has tried to institutionalize what is at bottom a work of spirit that resists institutionalization. In the process, it has in many respects lost its soul. That is why I prefer the term *laboratory*. A laboratory implies experimentation, trial and error, hands-on imagination. A laboratory by definition is a *search*, not a canned answer. A laboratory is humble therefore and not arrogant. A laboratory is something happening, not a place to sit passively and regurgitate answers. The arts dimension and the creativity dimension of the Awe Project is such a search – a search using tools and language of our postmodern times.

The YELLAWE version of a learning place will not compete with schools. Let the schools teach the 3 Rs as best they can. Let them accredit themselves as they do through the current bureaucracies. Let YELLAWE meet after school hours. The learning that goes on there will be so interesting and so alive and so valuable that students, who will be eager to participate after school hours, will return to school the next day with wonders to tell. They will be the viruses who change education. In addition, I would like to see foundations and philanthropists step forward and honour the young by paying those whose families are needy minimum wage to attend the learning laboratory. Better to be learning and yelling awe than to be flipping burgers that are bad for everyone's health.

The content of the laboratory has been laid out in this book. It consists of exploring questions of awe and of ancestors, of wisdom and of the 10 Cs of education. But the answers, the responses, will be unique and special, as diverse as the creative human mind itself, as individual students and teams of students respond with video, rap, poetry, break dancing, rituals, ceremonies, music, DJing and VJing, with images, and more. All students will learn the arts of contemplation, whether via martial arts, Tai Chi, *Vipassana* meditation, chant, movement, or other arts as meditation. Through these practices they will learn to quiet the reptilian brain so that their fuller brains, their mammal and intellectual/creative brains, might connect more deeply. All students will be marinated in the new cosmology and, with it, in skills and directions for living ecological and therefore sustainable lives.

To yell "Awe!" is a good thing. Especially in a time of boredom, acedia, apathy, taking for granted, and couchpotatoitis. We are yelling about the sad state of education in the world today, especially for the poor; and about how modern education is boring and is not meeting the needs of postmodern students. These needs include cosmology and contemplation; creativity and chaos; compassion and courage; critical consciousness and community; ceremony, celebration, and ritual; as well as character and chakra development.

To yell "Awe!" is the work of the fifth chakra, the prophetic chakra. It is what prophets do: They yell. They call out,

"Not this way, that way!" They speak out. It is so important today for youth and elders to be speaking out, calling out, and even *yelling* about the suicidal directions we are headed in; and about alternative directions that are salvific. The yelling is about awe.

No one who has tasted awe wants to keep it under a bushel. It is time to speak loudly about Ancestral Wisdom Education, in deeds as well as in words. Are there others out there listening? For the first time in history, 50 percent of humans are now under 16 years of age and 75 percent now live in cities. The young deserve and require new forms of education, in a language they can appreciate. Creativity and cosmology are its core. Edutainment is a valid form of education provided the content is substantive. Much depends upon our efforts at renewing education, including, ultimately, the survival of our species.

I await an educational revolution – one that is awe-based, ancestor-based, wisdom-based, and is based on the 10 Cs of education outlined in this book. Our ancestors are watching and waiting. And the souls of many not yet born.

APPENDIX A:
BASIC CURRICULUM FOR YELLAWE AFTER-SCHOOL HOURS PROJECT

1. The program will run from 3:00 p.m. to 6:00 p.m., Monday through Thursdays.

2. 3:00–3:30: Spiritual arts, such as Marriage of Heaven and Earth (Chi Gung), Tai Chi, and meditations or yoga, which teach self-discipline and centring through bodily awareness.

3. 3:30–4:10: Assistance with homework from the day.

4. 4:15–4:45: Teaching of the day. (This may include The New Cosmology, or Wonders of the Human Body, or How to Start Your Own Business, or Ecological Awareness and What We Can Do About It, or The Mysteries of Nature, etc.)

5. 4:50–6:00: Putting the teaching of the day into creative expression. (This means taking the content from the previous section and putting it into self-expression.) Forms of expression and skill-learning may include making video, making rap, creating ritual theatre, drumming, painting, creating comic books, and more.

Appendix B:
Lyrics from Professor Pitt's
DVD on the 10 Cs
Lyrics Copyright © Professor Pitt

1. Cosmology and Ecology

Yell ahh! Yell ahh! Well, first of all welcome to this educational
revolution, yell ahh acronym, Youth and Elders Learning
Laboratory of Ancestral Wisdom Education, watch it engulf the
world by the time we're done, introducing the Professor P.I.
double T and the thirty-book deep author M.A.T.T.H.E.W. Fox
peep the, what, you know the lecture that's conducted from the
mic into the speakers, but enough of the formality lets get on
with the true and living life reality. First class number one of
the ten Cs, cos, cosmology, well ask your self what does it
really mean to me, well let me explain this simply, the intimate
relationship between our human bodies, and the cosmos, plus
literally studies are finding out that our anatomies is made up
of star dust, so I'm related to every thing in the sky and every
thing that's true and living that meets my eye, and all of this
is absolutely nothing new quite frankly, it's ancient wisdom
cutting through the lies that say it's just cold mathematics
and distances that distances you from the reality, of your right to
live an intimate relationship with

Chorus:
cosmology…cos, cosmology…cos,

cosmology, an Australian theologian was lecturing in Africa, he

was being translated into Swahili, he said the number one spiritual problem

in his country was loneliness, what the African translator said,

please repeat the question, the translators huddled the other translators

came back to the microphone and said sorry in our language

there is no word for loneliness. What? Just what the hell are you

saying? How could this be, well this might be hard to understand

if you're married to this monstrous modern-day egotistical self-

centred human agenda hidden self-destruct plan that's gotcha

thinking and operating as if you're separate from the ocean, the

trees the animals the air the ozone layer, plus much more all connect

to become one big organism, a big living breathing body, my

mother Earth, and if us humans don't get a grip and get back to

playing our modest role instead of stupidly thinking that we're here

to control everything around us, if you think about it long

enough you'll realize that thought pattern is truly cancerous at this moment

I deeply connect to my cosmology, and let the mother Earth

herself speak freely through me, humans keep tripping, you

really want to hold a debate with a earth quake? Well, keep tripping,

you thinking you can swallow a tsunami? Well, keep tripping, you really

want to entertain a hurricane? Well come on and keep tripping keep

    tripping,

enough said Professor Pitt, go ahead. Another part of cosmology is when

    your

heart breaks and the whole universe can pour through cause as we

get broken in life the bigger works of the universe comes

through, so to every human being that's out there doing something mean to

    my

earth, I hope at this very moment and time that the

universe is pouring through your heart, meaning (yo) I hope it just got

broken (yo) shattered in half (yo) just so that we can live and so

that you can see how sensitive this situation is, you better

connect, you better connect to your cosmology.

2. Contemplation, Meditation (Kenois, emptying)

What up ya'll? It's the P.I. double T, Professor

that is. Yo I know sometimes your mind is just like a

raging ocean that just won't calm down but check the

technique and I'll show you how, cause this style

is meditation. So just breathe, just breathe.

Chorus:

This song is meditation, release the frustration

Breathe deep into your dontien*, dissolve the

tension your body's mostly water so see it as the ocean

Parts of you that resist relaxation are just

glaciers, blocks of ice, melt them

Focus on your breath ignore discomfort, or

pinpoint points of discomfort and breathe into them.

In this meditation your physical shell mirrors a

mountain, meaning you're not moving even the slightest inch

This is where the road or rather the rite of

passage that proclaims you the ancient warrior warlord triumphant one is

    patient

for whatever aches and itches, like everything in

life, is impermanent. Impermanence. What's impermanence?

like the ring of a bell, loud but still the resonance swells

into nothingness, meaning it's fading away the second

you're feeling it…unless you're holding onto it.

So, just breathe let it go, all the stress, and just

breathe let it go, all the stress just breathe let it go

all the stress, cause this is meditation ya'll, just breathe,

make sure your posture is straight bones resting on your bones

relax, count your breath and just breathe, just breathe

Chorus:

So all that stress, let it go, in one breath,

come on ya'll, just breathe, let the stress go, just

breathe let the stress go, cause this is meditation ya'll.

* "Dontien" refers to the third chakra.

3. Creativity

Whatever happened to honouring the same spirit that hovered
over the waters of creation?
Hovers over the creative mind of an artist in the midst of
the moment of creating another gem for the world, yes this
is for what we strive, nothing wrong with a song that'll
make the strong survive, or making love cooking raising
kings and queens, practising to heal a spleen or just
flowing with my chi now all of these exercise the gift of
creativity, not a single human being in this world wide
wide world lacks this ability, to co-create with the universe
personally, and give birth to our wisdom and truths
with such vibrancy, leaving mental pictures and images that
we paint through for others to see, whether it be
manifestations orientated in survival or sustainability for
all humanity on this W.O.R.L.D. like solar-energy-based
cities throughout this global society, JERKS, cause damn it
you better find a creative way to stop raping my mother
Earth my mother Earth with creativity.

Chorus:

As a species we see
We're at the tipping point of history
We each tap into our creativity
Or continue on this path of insanity

Where we won't complete our cycle, but end,

E.N.D.

Ahh that's deep

But that's real but that's real but that's

Ahh that's scary

But that's real but that's real but that's real

A yo I got a little fact for ya what up

Ahh that's real ahh that's real

Now let's get practical and contemplate on how we're going

to plunder these politicians' plans whose preposterous

version of healing the educational system is more exams

more exams more exams and on top of that more exams oh that

just kills the soul and imagination purely memorization but

what do these young minds have to offer this new world's

evolution, we better start asking this question instead of

making budget cuts on every thing that exercises our

creativity.

4. Chaos and Darkness

Chaos, Chaos, Chaos, wow! Sometimes I wonder, looking out

my third eye window, at a Westernized world that weighs anchor in

      anything

but wisdom, I see a nation that would rather wade in wicked

wretched flesh boring warm filled waters of forever

wanting more, never ending like a windmill constantly

Chaos, SPINNING Chaos, WINDING Chaos, SPIRALING Chaos,

WORLDWIND THAT'S Chaos, weaved inside a blood-filled whirlpool of

      warfare that leaves legions of welfare whimpering widows

with widowed-down souls,

cause they're left with fatherless families that's forced to

fight this four-headed, fanged, fiendish, fundamentalist fascist, multimedia,

      assassin,

assassin specialists, Chaos definition of religious fundamentalist mentality,

      "Now

there's only one way to honour GOD, and we got all the

answers, so you just get up on in line, or you're going to hell,"

Chaos. Definition of a political fascist mentality, basically it's

going to go like this, you're

going to join our empire or ...ahh... you can call it quits,

cause ain't no stopping this

Chaos, example Mussolini, Italy; Franco, Spain; Hitler,

Germany.

5. Compassion

So beautiful, so beautiful, my mother, my mother

Compassion, compassion

Thank you mother, thank you mother

Thank you father, thank you father

Universe for letting me live with compassion

The secret word for the universe female energy

Male energy

It's all about healing, all about living, all

about feeling, all about bringing

the balance between your body and mind that

intertwines your heart and your head

The word for compassion in Arabic and in Hebrew

comes from the word womb

To deny the power of that is like a welcome mat

to a tomb

So I respect that if I'm really down for life and living

I'm really down for honouring all our women

Our mothers, our sisters, our woman

Compassion

And let's not forget compassion itself within

ourselves

Wow, tell me what woman don't love when a man can

gently caress her whole being

and genuinely care for her well-being

This is compassion a feminine energy

But yo don't trip

Balance this with the male energy rugged individualism

the ability to endure and

drop emotionalism get with the realism

focus with the task at hand and take control, wooooo

But there must be balance or we're just

dangerous to ourselves and others

without compassion.

Like Taoism, the yin and yang

thank you universe for letting me live with compassion

Our greatest capacity as a species, compassion, compassion, compassion,

Compassion…

You can reject everything else, religion, ideology, all received wisdom but

we cannot escape the necessity of love and compassion. For with this

you can see through the facade. Every face is the face of GOD an image

a reflection. A mirror a nod from ALLAH to BUDDHA, RAH, JAH, YAH

 WEH…

All the same. It all comes down to universal compassion.

6. Courage (Ballad of the Angels' War Dance)

This is the ballad of the angels' war dance…

It seems to me that the last couple centuries that

we been in the earth's night

where those with halos had to lay low, but yo, we're dawning on the

    earth's day and I that is we that is I is here to say ring the alarm

Wake up, come on ya'll we've got demons to kill

There they go – get'em!

Those cancerous entities that continuously cause catastrophe

Chaos carnage and mass confusion. But no more half-stepping…

There they go. Let's get'em! First on the list, who fear?

No more will you hold hostage this whole hemisphere. Line'em up we're

doing a fly by, say bye-bye.

To the earth's night, in comes the day where angels play in the glory

of the cleansing rain that whistles in the wind provided by decapitated

    demons. While their body fluids are sprayin, dissolving the fear deeply

implanted in your mind being decaying, giving birth to courage

Or should we say awaken your natural original nature that's used as

    weapons to slaughter the slithering slugs that pollute your mind, move

    within yourself to find your offence, defence metaphysical weapons

Pick em up!!

Quan-Dow

Panabus

Spears,

Panutas

Dart rope

Curses

Shields

Hollow point projectile

Crossbows

Barongs

Deer horns

Bolisongs

Universe the harp

Three section guillotines for those with three heads our

slumber is over, it's time to put heads to bed

This is the ballad of the angels' war dance…

Big brother dragon!

Hey! You ever felt a dark cloud surrounding you

Be aware the end is near. That's my shadow…

Within me the energy of we welcome the opportunity for combat.

Matter of fact to be exact, set free… patiently we've been waiting for

centuries. To pull wigs back and break backs to make sacroiliac

necklaces ripped straight out of carcasses with bare hands in the midst

of the dance that divinely dismantles dozens of dirty demons that's

been daily dealing dastardly deeds, raining supreme, metaphysically

entering the human M.I.N.D. convincing their bodies to make moves to

lose their souls but no more…

War dance, war dance, minds goes in a trance

All we see is geometric diagrams

Like holograms 3-D in their circumference

wrapped around the damned doomed to dance with the body alignment.

"re-arranger"... Uh Oh... Oh my GOD, Danger...

A yo, big brother dragon do you recall when we sat in the

circle of energy when before time began

we all swore we'd come back throughout the centuries in these

flesh body suits of man and woman hallo and wings unseen but felt?

Come step into the centre of the sun plastic, we'll see who melts... As

this present proceeds to become history unfolds...

7. Critical Consciousness & Judgment

This class will let me explain critical

I'm at a cross street

Consciousness

I better look both ways to make sure I see the

end of this day

Judgment

There's no cars coming so I move, so I move

Critical

I am speeding

Consciousness

And there's a cop behind me

Judgment

I slow down, man I slow down

Critical

I'm at a gas station and a hooded character

creeps up

from behind

raising a Glock 9, saying break yourself and

give

me mine

Consciousness

This could be life or death and whatever is in my

pockets,

compared to my life, man, is worthless

Judgment

I crack a smile and stand tall

empty out my pockets and say take it all

I hope you have a ball

All I'm really trying to do is see tomorrow

And I do, and I do

Critical

I'm taking a beautiful woman out on a date

My intentions at the end of the night

I don't have to masturbate

Consciousness

Man, in this game there's so many

sexually transmitted diseases

that will give you the sneezes

that don't stop 'til you drop dead

Judgment

I'll buy a condom, I'll buy a condom, I'll buy a

condom

Critical

Man I've been smoking weed non-stop

And drinking every night 'til I'm drunk

Every night to the point my woman

Is looking at me in disgust

And saying I ain't right and she's right

Consciousness

Sometimes is real thick, hard to deal with

I have to face it

I'm a weed-head-alcoholic and I need help

When? Today

Judgment

I go join NA and AA today

So I can get my life right and see a brighter day

Critical, consciousness, judgment

I just think, man I just think, think about it!!

Chorus:

You better think!

8. Community

We must find a way, we must find a way

to reunite history and rekindle community in this

perplex matrix of complex world communities of cities that are

lost, long to be found but when shall we be found and

find a nest of indigenous ways to install in our culture

something to offset these venomous vultures and their

vulturous ways that eat away in decay at our

spiritual immunities, the cause and effect the

crumbling of a world insanity that ultimately leads to

the end of humanity. Panic button pushed, someone elected

Bush. Is this the portrait of Christian to rob,

destroy and rape the holy land??

We must find a way, we must find a way…

to reunite history and rekindle community…

It seems to me, the Professor P.I. double T, that the loss

of community began when we lost sight that beneath

these body suits lie souls of blue flaming and divine

light that throughout infinity has always been

intricately and continuously connected through our

unconscious purpose, perfectly placed pieces to the

puzzle of universal peace, Chaos included. From the

star charts to the universe's Rolex, we are all on time,

from the doorways of temperament that we choose to

walk through, to get done what we need to do…

Leos

Aries

Sagittarius

Ox's

Dragons

Monkeys

Roosters

Taurus

Bores

Virgos

Horses

Capricorns

Libras

Snakes

Rabbits

Geminis

Dogs

Scorpios

Tigers

And on down the line, keep in mind our cosmic

connection to everything and community we will find…

NOTE: *(An overall message in my ancient tongue that is basically apologizing to the feminine side of the universe as well as promising the masculine side of the universe that we as a species will honour our mother compassion, as well as reconnect to our modest role in the universe. Respecting all the other parts.)*

9. Ceremony, Celebration, and Ritual

Ceremony, celebration, ritual, spirit,

Ritual, celebration, ceremony, mind, ceremony, celebration,

Ritual, body, ritual, celebration, ceremony, move...

Spirit mind body in the act of ceremony relax attach and

become one intention whether it be the ceremony, Christmas

or Kwanza, a wedding, a funeral, or a bar mitzvah. The ceremony

the gathering of a community family into the we that is I that

is we. Energy, it only takes one seed of divinity to grow

the everlasting vibrant tree of life that springs from the

soil of respect of our past, an honouring our ancestors that

long ago past on a responsibility to keep on progressing

manifestating stay'in forever thirsty for lessons. Now

with this spirit mind body move mode on we move on to

celebration. Celebration, spirit mind body party body rock

celebration move mind body like ritual sooth if I prove to my

elders that they can leave this earth for me to rule with integrity, use

my mental tool, opposite of a fool. To weld my compassion

with courage for my community, manoeuvre with creativity

critical consciousness and judgment for my arsenal to dance

with Chaos is heaven sent contemplation, meditation, Zen,

for my continuous chakra development that will continuously

keep me connected to my cosmology.

All this unfolds in front of the babies next to my youth

next to my peers next to my elders my right of passage

complete, victory!! My community now honours me through

ritual, celebration, and ceremony, ceremony, celebration, ritual, spirit,
    ritual,
celebration, ceremony, mind, ceremony, celebration, ritual, body,
ritual, celebration, ceremony, move…
We all need rituals at birth at death at puberty at marriage
at divorce at retirement refirement at graduations and
healings it's all part of being humans and animals all
seeking receiving gifts of ceremonies that recharge us heal
us energize us amaze us they release our best capacities of
compassion and service, honouring teaching learning,
honouring beginnings endings. Remember to reconnect with our
ancestors. Usher them among us.

10. Character and Chakra Development

Chakras, what are they? Where are they? What

purpose do they serve?

Well let's go on a field trip through my mind

connect to the energetic anatomy of the human

body and see what we find

Ok, who am I?

I'm located at the bottom of your spine

My sole purpose in life, call it my job

is to produce your pride and connect through

movement to the earth and all vibrations of the universe.

First if I had to suggest a simile

to get to the centre of the point

simply I would say that I'm an antenna

Would you really get the point?

If I unfold the…

fact that your sacroiliac is a tail

Therefore this is why we find all animals

with tails to be more sensitive to the unseen

Now the dark side of me can be detected instantly

For this is when the presence of pride

goes through the intense transformation that twists into

arrogance and this is ugly for real

But before I reveal my identity I must let you

see I'm…connected to sub chakras in your knees and

feet and this is why indigenous people pray on their

feet, they dance for when their heels get hot the

energy flows upwards and opens us up

Check-in chakra number one!

Wow I love sex! With more than a passion

to be exact for you… oooooooo I produce passion…

Man not to mention one of my occupations give irresistible

needs to reproduce life.

In the name of the human species and this is a

reality the dark side of me

is using lust as a weapon don't you see

Or preaching of oppression and fear of L-U-S-T

I'm through…

Check-in chakra number two!!!

See I'm famous they call me the Dontien one of my job

titles, well I'm your groundin. If you were a boat then I'm

your anchor, look at me as the

well that springs your positive use of anger and

moral outrage and please let's not even speak of the page

of the dark side of me

that springs from the well of violence and rage

Murderous, murderous

Enough of this enough of this

Check in your center your battery

chakra number three!!

I am your courage

that which does not pump cool-aid, your heart

Plus I smash ignorance apart with

compassion and forgiveness my strongest weapon and

please make this clear. I behead while draw and

quartering my archenemy: fear. And if your first move is

with me, then you have no fear, for at that moment you are

in the universe's core

Check-in, check-in chakra number four!!

Well, while you've been on this field trip I hope you

have been taking notes

Me? Well, moving right up the ladder I reside in

your throat…

So I would say watch what you say

pack with universal pull. I'm powerful for you play with your life why test??

Speaking out to the universe, what you say just may manifest.

This is the power that I have… HEY, think about it.

What kind of power do you try to activate when

you pray, ME!! But mostly, everybody turns the power switch off!

To the point where it's almost permanent.

Never to feel this perfect potential

Of this endless potent power that I could give

You, word is bond… Let me let you in on what must be the most

forgotten… universal law, cause and effect, speaking of a feminine

energy in disrespect disconnects the divine energy

that powers me.

Dig that...

Think about it.

How many rap albums have stolen your power?

Forced you to disconnect while

chanting anthems of feminine disrespect

Think about it, whose lives

Check-in chakra number five!!

Critical consciousness and judgment blow!!!

Just one of the many job titles that I hold. I'm chillin at the

centre of the beginning of your forehead, and at the end of your

eyebrow. Somehow people started referring to me as your third eye.

See I, see the I that is we that is I, as well as see into the next

dimensions be with universally wise eyes. Or at least let them feel

them through intuition now I just got to mention, I balance what's known

as both sides of the brain. This is what keeps you

from going insane. The left is the critical, more analytical

dark side of me well, that's being judgmental. The right side of the

brain, the left would call insane. Cause I don't pass judgment. And

even understand the unseen intuition. I'm just checking-in chakra number

beeeeeepp!!!!

Ha ha ha. Who am I? What rhymes with heaven who am I? What

rhymes with eleven? Who am I? What rhymes with Teflon? Who

am I? The same number minus, the double 0 of James Bonds. I carry on

the riddle to let

you know I number da na na na na na na na. I number seven, of the

chakras you see. My power connects span beyond the seven seas. The

   power

of all that is we. Call it community. Over the centuries they

nicknamed me the crown. So I guess that you can call me royalty.

The dark side of me, well, that's envy. Anything that keeps you from

connecting to the next human being or the universe, disperse!! Class is

over, do your research. Wisdom, flame ignited, I hope you enjoyed your

field trip.

DVD Credits
Special thanks

Mother and Father Universe

Matt Fox

Tsomo

John Kiefer

Ted Richards

Andrew Jones

Avery Williams

Steve Snider

LaTonia Miller

(Leo Dragon) Jeremy Hughes

Running Bear

Eddy Deutsche

Raheem & Elisha Colas

Sarah Colas

Esra Gold

Si-Fu Sherman Lee

2232 MLK

Alex Gray

Robert Corbett

Cody

Media Circus

Friends of Creation Spirituality

Pictures – Artwork for Chakra Development provided by
Alex Grey

All songs written, recorded, filmed, edited and directed by
Phillip "Professor Pitt" Colas

Camera Work by
Esra Gold
Raheem & Elisha Colas
Naim Thomas-Ortiz
LaTonia Miller
Cody

Myspace/profressorpitt.com
Jeremy Hughes of the I N Team Production
www.myspace/inteamproduction.com

Ballad of the Angels' War Dance recorded by
Robert Corbett

All songs (except Ballad of the Angels' War Dance) recorded at
P.I. double T.V. Studios

ACKNOWLEDGEMENTS

I want to thank Maria Montessori for her profound insights into educating children, and also the many practitioners of the Waldorf school tradition whose work is equally inspiring. I wish to acknowledge the many, many co-workers I have taught with over the years, while attempting to reinvent education, first at ICCS in Chicago, and then at ICCS in Oakland, and finally at the University of Creation Spirituality in Oakland (now Wisdom University). Teachers, fellow administrators, staff, board members – all have been my fellow-learners. With special appreciation to M. C. Richards, whose lifelong adventure with Rudolf Steiner and alternative education so married with creation spirituality programs. And above all, I thank the *students* whose deep but spontaneous response to the pedagogy taught me so much.

And thanks to Professor Pitt, whose putting of my thoughts to rap and video has been a deep learning experience for me and I trust for others. And to Dr. Mark Gonnerman of Stanford University, for his feedback and valuable criticism of my original manuscript.

I also wish to acknowledge the many teachers in my life who have made such a difference in my love of learning and the educing of others' learning, including but not limited to scholars cited in this book such as Ernest Becker, Rabbi Abraham Heschel, Tom Hayden, and David Korten. With a special thanks to my brother, Tom Fox, and his trust of children's minds, and the wisdom of the arts and hands-on activities that were so evident so early in his teaching career – he remains one of my important teachers.

– Matthew Fox

ENDNOTES

Preface: A Crisis Called Education

1 Bill Gates, "Why We Must Redesign Our High Schools," *San Francisco Chronicle*, March

3, 2005, B9.

Chapter 1: Education: Gift or Punishment, Blessing or Curse?

1 Ernest Becker, *Beyond Alienation: A Philosophy of Education for the Crisis of Democracy* (New York: George Braziller, 1967), 254.

2 Matthew Fox, *Original Blessing* (New York: Tarcher, 2000).

3 David C. Korten, *The Great Turning: From Empire to Earth Community* (San Francisco: Berrett-Koehler Publishers, copy-edited version, 2005), 248f.

4 Cited in Becker, *Beyond Alienation*, 59f.

5 Ibid., 258.

6 Cited in Mark Gonnerman, "On the Path, Off the Trail: Gary Snyder's Education and the Making of American Zen" (Department of Religious Studies, Stanford University: PhD Dissertation, October, 2003), 417.

7 Ibid., 439.

8 Becker, *Beyond Alienation*, 18.

9 Ibid., 126.

10 Ibid., 212.

11 Sharif Abdullah, *Creating a World that Works for All* (San Francisco: Berrett-Koehler Publishers, 1999).

12 Robert Freeman, "Are We Buying Our

'McStudent' Lie?" *San Francisco Chronicle*, January 18, 2005, B7.

Chapter 2: The A.W.E. Project: Awe-Based Education

1 Becker, *Beyond Alienation*, 220.

2 Abraham Heschel, *Man Is Not Alone: A Philosophy of Religion* (New York: Farrar, Straus & Giroux, 1951), 37.

3 Matthew Fox and Rupert Sheldrake, *Natural Grace* (New York: Doubleday Image, 1997), 18.

4 Ibid., 21.

5 See Sondra Barrett, *Cellular Mysteries* (unpublished MS, 2003), 29–45 and Donald E. Ingber, "The Architecture of Life," *Scientific American*, January 1998, 48–57.

6 See Matthew Fox, *Sins of the Spirit, Blessings of the Flesh* (New York: Tarcher, 1999), chapters 1–4.

7 Gaston Bachelard, *The Poetics of Space* (Boston: Beacon Press, 1994), 193.

8 Ibid., 195.

9 Becker, *Beyond Alienation*, 239.

10 David Korten, "Money vs. Wealth," *YES!*, Summer, 1997.

11 Becker, *Beyond Alienation*, 256.

12 Ibid., 192f.

13 Paulo Freire, *Pedagogy of the Oppressed* (New York: Continuum Books, 1970).

14 *San Francisco Chronicle*, January 27, 2005, A13.

15 Cited in Jim Garrison, *Civilization and the Transformation of Power* (New York: Paraview Press, 2000), 260.

16 Ibid., 258.

Chapter 3: A: Ancestor-Based

[1] Cited in Catherine Hammond, ed., *Creation Spirituality and the Dreamtime* (Newtown NSW, Australia, 1991), 93f.

[2] Ibid., 89.

[3] Cited in Matthew Fox, *Wrestling with the Prophets* (New York: Tarcher, 2003), 146f.

[4] Gabrielle Uhlein, *Meditations with Hildegard of Bingen* (Santa Fe: Bear & Co., 1983), 30, 32, 41.

Chapter 4: W: Wisdom-Based

[1] Peter Kingsley, *In the Dark Places of Wisdom* (Inverness, CA: The Golden Sufi Center, 1999), 31f.

[2] Ibid., 35.

[3] Abraham Joshua Heschel, *The Insecurity of Freedom* (New York: Schocken Books, 1966), 42–43.

[4] Tom Hayden, *Street Wars: Gangs and the Future of Violence* (New York: The New Press, 2004), 311.

[5] Ibid., 332.

[6] Ibid., 318.

[7] Kingsley, *Dark Places of Wisdom*, 213.

[8] See Matthew Fox, *Sheer Joy: Conversations with Thomas Aquinas on Creation Spirituality* (New York: Jeremy Tarcher, 2003), 37, 242.

Chapter 5: E: Education – 10 Cs to Balance the 3 Rs

[1] Cited in Alex Gerber Jr., *Wholeness: On Education, Buckminster Fuller, and Tao*, (Kirkland, Washington: Gerber Educational Resources, 2001), 47-50

[2] Ibid., 80.

[3] Ibid., 83.

[4] Estelle Frankel, *Sacred Therapy: Spiritual Jewish Teachings on Emotional Healing and Inner Wholeness* (Boston: Shambhala, 2003), 2f.

[5] Julian Guthrie, "On Schooling: Schools Reach for Yoga to Calm and Collect Students," *San Francisco Chronicle*, B1.

[6] Charles Burack, "Returning Meditation to Education," *Tikkun* (September/October, 1999), 41–46.

[7] Cited in Matthew Fox, *One River, Many Wells: Wisdom Springing from Global Faiths* (New York: Tarcher, 2000), 416.

[8] Personal Correspondence from Phil Barton, January 3, 2006.

[9] Carl Pope, "Our Government Can Do Something about the Weather," *San Francisco Chronicle*, October 2, 2005, C5.

[10] See Ralph Abraham, *Chaos Gaia, Eros* (San Francisco: HarperSanFrancisco, 1994).

[11] Cited in Fox, *One River, Many Wells*, 417.

[12] See Matthew Fox, *Creativity: Where the Divine and the Human Meet* (New York: Tarcher, 2002), 173.

[13] Jim Garrison, *The Darkness of God: Theology after Hiroshima* (Grand Rapids, Michigan: William B. Eerdmans, 1982), 68.

[14] Ibid., 69.

[15] Ibid.

[16] Ibid., 91.

[17] Becker, *Beyond Alienation*, 39f.

[18] Ibid.

[19] Korten, *The Great Turning*, 235.

[20] Becker, *Beyond Alienation*, 268.

[21] Ibid., 233.

[22] Ibid., 268.

[23] Ibid., 276.

[24] Ibid.

[25] Ibid., 277.

[26] Gerber, *Wholeness*, 85.

[27] Ibid., 86.

[28] Korten, *The Great Turning*, 254.

[29] Garrison, *Civilization and the Transformation of Power*, 303.

[30] This explanation of the chakras is elaborated on in Matthew Fox, *Sins of the Spirit, Blessings of the Flesh*, chapters 8–14.

[31] Becker, *Beyond Alienation*, 67.

[32] Ibid., 78.

[33] Ibid., 191.

About the Author

Matthew Fox has been an educator for 35 years, during which he has been designing, teaching, and administering programs for undergraduate, master's, and doctoral students. Early in his teaching career, he set out to consciously reinvent the way we do education, convinced as he was that the heart and lower charkas, along with creativity and intuition, were sidelined by mainstream educational pedagogy. The results with adults were very powerful.

Now in his 66th year, he is eager to take the lessons learned from teaching and designing pedagogy for adults to younger people and is teaming up with a rapper/media artist and kung fu practitioner, Professor Pitt, to launch an after-school program in Oakland, California, called YELLAWE, described in this book.

Fox is convinced that postmodern children require and deserve postmodern forms of education, and that the pedagogy he has seen work wonders with adults will work even greater wonders with children. He believes that education will most likely be reinvented by inner-city children, who are most losing out at the hands of the tired, modern forms of education that are still in vogue today. He has provided an alternative model that does not compete with the school system (since it meets after school hours), he feels that such a mirror will provide valuable new ideas to educational practice and philosophy.

Matthew Fox is author of 27 books on spirituality and culture and its reinvention. He resides in Oakland, California, and holds two master's degrees from American universities, and a doctorate from the Institut Catholique de Paris. He lectures widely around the world, teaches part-time at Stanford University, and is a visiting lecturer at various universities throughout North America. His books have been translated into 42 languages and have received numerous awards. He is recipient of the *Peace Abbey Conscience Award.*

More of his work can be seen at <u>www.matthewfox.org</u> and he can be reached for talks and workshops alone or with Professor Pitt at 33dennis@sbcglobal or at <u>www.speakingmatters.org</u> or by phone at 510-835-0655.

About the DVD Composer

Professor Pitt (a.k.a. Philip T. Colas) is a 32-year-old African American rapper, hip hop artist, martial arts practitioner, teacher, and filmmaker who has produced two films of a trilogy around the theme of "Kung Fu Meets Hip Hop." He is also a television journalist and music producer. Pitt's films are *The Hip Hop Dynasty* and *Hip Hop Dynasty Part II* produced by Dirty Lenz Films. Pitt was executive producer and artistic director for both films, as well as actor and film editor. His most recent album, *The Organic Equation*, touches on themes such as ancestral roots, meditation, and social change.

His goal in working with youth is to provide an alternative hip hop that focuses on youth development and community building, without the influence of the mainstream corporate image that exploits the medium. Together, he and Matthew Fox are working to establish an after-hours school program for inner-city youth in Oakland, California, based on the educational philosophy of YELLAWE and The A.W.E. Project. They also do an intergenerational, interracial program together called "Hip Hop Lecture," which speaks to the themes of this book.